Disillusionment: The Doorway to Present Moment Clarity

By Roy Melvyn

Disillusionment: The Doorway to Present Moment Clarity
By Roy Melvyn

Summa Iru Publishing
Broomfield, Colorado 80020

The stolen glances, broken threads
The visions looming in our heads
The years spent running parallel
To everything that might of been
No longer possible to hide
The feeling welling up inside
Ain't never been this close before
Ain't never felt so far away
When a moment
A moment changes everything
When a moment
A moment changes everything
When a moment, it changes everything
The summer sky is blushing pink
The heart is running out of sync
Could this just be the day, I think
When anything is possible
Well, hey now you've been here before
To see your face and slam the door
And waiting for the floor to drop
Feel like time is standing still
When a moment
A moment changes everything
When a moment
A moment changes everything
When a moment, it changes everything

David Gray

Table of Contents

Dedication

To all the seers, sages, and mystics over the centuries who saw the Unseen and sought to express what they came to understand.

Disclaimer

It is within the very nature of the English language to create duality, to set up the distinction between subject and object, between noun and verb. I can only talk about what is accessible to thinking and language. Almost every sentence written or spoken reinforces this duality.
But where something greater is concerned, I can only state that it is beyond all definition. The only way to know what it is like to be red is to be red.
Those who seek to parse the words contained in this book will no doubt find fault with them. This is unavoidable.
However, the word is not the thing. Those who become fixated on the finger pointing at the sun, never see the sun.

Introduction

Welcome.

I feel it is important to begin by saying that I am not intent on convincing you of anything. All that I want to do is to present an alternative point of view and to share what I have come to understand. Should you decide to pursue the same lines of inquiry that I took up, I am confident that you will find it productive.

Next, I want to state that I have nothing to give to you that you don't already have. As such, there's nothing you'll get from me. I prefer to frame it this way: you believe that you've lost your reading glasses and you've asked me to help you locate them. All I'm saying is "Have a look; they're sitting on your nose".

As you read these pages, you are faced with 3 options:

Reject them, continue to believe what you believe and move on. This will be the majority response.

Without questioning, embrace them fully as you have embraced 1+1=2 or the notion that you are a male or female. Then, live accordingly.

Investigate for yourself whether or not my viewpoint is valid.

Readers who are expecting to be "taken beyond" or "go beyond" will be disappointed. There is no beyond to go to.

There is only before: before beliefs, before ideas and concepts, before stories and histories, before imaginations, before words, before language, before projections, before emotions, before sensations, before feelings, before love and hate, before good and evil, before every this and every that.

The models generated by the biochemical processes in our brains constitute the reality we've come to know. None of us can ever be completely sure that the world really is as it appears, or if our minds have unconsciously imposed a misleading pattern on the data.

After looking at life from different perspectives, I eventually realized that many of the beliefs I had taken for granted about the nature of reality were simply mistaken.

Change is not easy. We crave the familiar, the routine, and the predictable because we are wired to the familiar through our environment. Continuous exposure to our routine reality only wires us to be more habitual and predictable. It's living in a loop.

We have caged ourselves in a box of our own repetitive thinking, rethinking, acting, and reacting. Our limited thinking is literally our limited frame of mind.

Our beliefs shape, influence, and even control everything we think, do, and say about the world. The power of belief is so strong that we typically form our beliefs first. We then construct a rationale for holding those beliefs after the fact.

We form our beliefs for a variety of subjective, emotional, and psychological reasons in the context of environments created by family, friends, colleagues, and culture. After forming our beliefs we then defend, justify, and rationalize them with a host of intellectual reasons and rational explanations. Beliefs come first, explanations and rationalizations for those beliefs follow.

From sensory data flowing in through the senses, the brain naturally begins to look for and find patterns, and then infuses those patterns with meaning as it relates to the self-center. Once our brains connect the dots of our world into meaningful patterns of belief, we look for and find confirming evidence to support them and employ a host of cognitive biases that ensures we are always right.

The only escape from this trap is the use of a scientific method which bypasses the cognitive biases that so cripple our grasp of the reality that actually exists.

Others have been telling us how things are for our entire life. We gladly buy this hearsay because easy answers for life's tough questions are quite popular. Most of us prefer to avoid the challenge of performing the investigation ourselves.

To think outside the box is to utilize new modes of thinking. Rather than working from routine processes, from consideration of "what has been" thought, it is from consideration of "what might be" thought. Normally, the brain must filter out most of what assaults it; it's simply too much. When we make an affirmative shift in the willingness of the brain to filter out what it had previously considered to be extraneous or unimportant, new insights open up.

Non-investigation is the thread on which all beliefs are strung. It is like darkness in a closed room. It is apparently there. But when the doors and windows are opened, where does the darkness go? It goes nowhere, because it was never there.

What is false cannot withstand rigorous investigation. Its life relies on the absence of scrutiny. Doubt is the actual terrain of this investigative process.

Our need to believe highlights this truth: we just don't know.

Everything we believe was believed before we arrived here. We weren't born with beliefs; we acquired them.

What we do not know and what we merely believe enslaves us. There is no need to discover new truisms; simply recognize what is false as false.

The following brief monologues and dialogues will engage you and challenge you to look more deeply at your certainties.

The truth of it is that these very same certainties are the only obstacle.

Terms

I'd like to start with a bit of clarification.

In my writings and conversations, I repeatedly reference three concepts: self-consciousness, consciousness, and awareness. They are not interchangeable.

Self consciousness is the source of individuality. It is the support of I, me, and their derivatives.

Consciousness is the source of duality and multiplicity. It is the support of all things. Self consciousness emerges from it.

Awareness is the source of consciousness. It is its own support. It is the Background against which the foreground appears, the Changeless upon which all change arises, the Stillness upon which all movement occurs.

A few other buzzwords, if I may:

The brain-in-the-body, of and by itself, is inert. Life force enervates and animates it. Consciousness provides the sentience that is required. This pair I refer to as the Complex and the brain-in-the-body serves as its instrument.

The brain-in-the-body, its processes and actions and the narrative that forms about them constitute what I call the Composite. Reification of the Composite is the idea of an individual entity with agency, independence of action.

Mind is not a separate thing. It is not a noun; it's a verb. Mind is what the brain does.

Critical Thinking

It is not infrequent that I begin my talks with some comments about critical thinking.

Things are not always what they seem and it is this very recognition that is perhaps the key feature of the critical thinker's approach.

The brain imparts reality to whatever it perceives. To say that something seems real doesn't have any meaning. Everything seems real, doesn't it? However, the truth is that the world is a deceptive place, not by intention, but inherently.

Having such a worldview casts a wide net which allows us to incorporate a broader recognition of the deceptive nature of the world. It forces us to acknowledge that:

We are often unaware of the constraints imposed on our perceptions by the socially correct forces outside of us and the DNA-based forces inside us. Our cognitive biases literally hamstring us.

We are often sorely ignorant of our ignorance. Interestingly, the more incompetent we are, the more likely we are to overestimate our competence. How else could 18% of college students believe that they are in the top 5% in their class or that 78% of all drivers believe themselves to be above average?

Whereas issues frequently appear black-and-white, they usually consist of a whole lot of grays.

We are more likely to be misled by people who sincerely believe what they are saying than by liars. Conviction sells and we're anxious to be sold.

Last, self-deception is an even bigger impediment to our understanding than deception by others.

Since it is so easy to misperceive, a critical thinker is not quick to take things at face value, is suspicious of certainties and absolutes, and is not easily swayed by conventional wisdom.

In other words, critical thinkers are unwilling to accept the brain's default posture that everything is true. They understand that their knowledge on any subject is fallible, likely incomplete, and subject to change.

Developing a solid understanding of the way things are means that one's foundational assumptions will be disturbed, many will be overturned. Too, toes will be stepped on and, from my personal experience, members of an audience may bolt from the room.

This type of thinking requires traits such as:

Being unwilling to subordinate one's thinking to the commonly held views that demand they be swallowed whole.

Refusing to dismiss possible merits in ideas that reflexively feel wrong. Being capable of saying, "I don't know" at the risk of appearing lacking in intelligence.

Being willing to change one's mind.................and then change it again.

This process of subjecting ideas and concepts to intellectual due diligence can require more integrity, humility, tolerance of uncertainty, and courage than most of us can summon.

However, that must not dissuade us.

I would argue that those who traverse this road to true understanding are met by twin toll collectors: paradox and confusion. The toll charged for passing through to the other side into clarity is steep; it is everything we think we know.

You are your own final authority. Don't take anyone's statements as fact, including my own.

Take Me There

Q: Can you take me to the place where you have arrived?

I can take you to the doorway, but you'll have to walk through it yourself. Fair enough?

Q: OK, but it sounds like you're asking us to give up our entire identity. Am I right?

I'll leave that for you to decide. Ready to proceed?

Q: Sure.

OK, what we know is that your identity is an ever-changing basket of concepts. The way you saw yourself a year ago, a decade ago, is not the same as it is today. You see that, don't you?

Q: I do.

This identity consists of:

Your body as a composite entity along with its sensations.

Your personality.

Your mental processes, everything that constitutes your mind.

Your numerous life roles as Anglo-Saxon Protestant, American, man, spouse, parent, child, employee, lover, etc.

Your ownership of possessions or projections, such as your car, your house, your appearance, your ideas

Your ownership of your circumstances, interpersonal relationships, history………. in sum, everything comprising your "story"

Have I omitted anything?

Q: I don't think so.

If I strip away everything you consider to be your identity, do you continue to exist?

(pause) Yes, I exist.

You exist; there is existence. No one needs to tell you this.

You are aware that you exist; there is awareness. Correct?

Q: Yes.

So there is existence and awareness.

You can say "I am aware"; there is awareness of awareness.

So, we have three aspects of being, without John coming into the picture. And without these three, there is no John.

Q: Yes.

These three are then the support of whatever we hold to be John.

Now, let's move to the awareness of the organism John. There is awareness of the perceptions that come thru the organism and there is awareness of the conceptions or thoughts that appear to the organism. All this is going on in the absence of any identity, agreed?

Q: Don't I have to believe I'm John for all this to occur?

Not at all. The phenomenon John is happening and you are aware of it.

Q: Oh................ I follow.

Then why pick up the identity again? The awareness, the perceptions and the conceptions are all occurring as before. There are no problems; only some aspect of the identity has problems.

Being nothing in particular is the default state, so to speak. In words, it is "I am". This "I am" is the universal magnet; it can be attached to virtually anything. In so doing, we create for example, I am happy, I am famous, I am beautiful, I am this body, etc.

However, once these attachments are established, the purity that is prior to any identity becomes obscured.

So, why not remain as you are without the identity? This is the doorway.

Are you ready to walk through it?

Trust

Q: Is it OK to change teachers? I have done this several times. Why not change?

Teachers are like mile markers. It is natural to move on from one to another. Each tells you the direction. What is innate in you is your ultimate teacher; it is the road itself.

Q: I'm always worried that my teacher will be angry if I leave.

The teacher has a secret. She or he knows that you really don't need them. If the teacher doesn't make this secret an open secret, if they don't remind you of this, something is amiss.

From a commercial point of view, teachers need paying students. The economics is straightforward. As such, there exists a vested interest in establishing a dependency on the teacher.

Q: Are you suggesting I be distrustful?

Trust cannot be blindly offered. Trust, then test. If all is OK, trust more, test more. Rinse and repeat.

Q: What about the behavior of the teacher? Must it be exemplary?

Teachers can vary between the saint-like and markedly less than that. It is the teaching that matters, not the teacher.

You get a letter that makes you laugh or cry. It is not the postman who does it. Why make him responsible for the quality of the message?

There is no way a true teacher is supposed to be.

What you can see, what you attempt to judge, is only the personality of this object you are calling teacher. Because you imagine yourself to be a person, you view the teacher as a person too. He or she appears to be somewhat different, maybe better informed or more powerful.

Q: Do you see yourself as a teacher?

I was made into one by being called so. I have a point of view, one among many. This viewpoint is like a suit of clothes; you try it on. If you like it, you wear it. If it's not comfortable, if it doesn't feel right, you don't.

Q: What, then, do you really do?

What can I really do? I can point to the sky but it is up to you to discern the stars. I can give you the address, I can take you to the door, but you have to go inside. I can provide the wind, but you have to hoist the sail.

Q: My life is hectic: two jobs, a wife and three small kids. It just seems to me that there's no time to do what you suggest.

No time is required to stand outside of time.
You may not now be able to change your circumstances, but your attitude can change. Start with a single, small step.
Be willing to see things differently.

The Quick Version

Q: Look, I don't have a lot of time. So give me only the salient stuff of what you have to offer.

OK, may I infer that you're looking to find the key that opens the door to happiness and contentment?

Q: Yes you can.

Well, there's good news and there's bad news.

The bad news is that I don't have the key.

The good news is that the door is unlocked and already open.

Q: Fine; so what do I have to do?

It is not what you have to do that is pivotal. It is what you have to stop doing that makes the difference.

The Current State of Affairs

For those of you that haven't been here before, I'd like to give you some sense of what this is all about.

All of us have spent almost the entirety of our lives believing that we are individuals, that we are personalities with pasts and, hopefully, futures.

Most of us, however, are dissatisfied with the way things are. We believe that there could be something more. Some are just beginning to search for it. Others have been searching unsuccessfully for months, years, and decades.

Why is this so? Maybe it's because you've been looking in the wrong place.

We believe that we know what we are. I challenge that. I don't believe that most of us do. What we believe is mere hearsay, told to us over and over by our parents, peers, teachers and society.

We've never taken the time to look and see for ourselves. That's what we do here.............. and we do that by removing what we aren't and seeing what remains. It is the same method as the sculptor uses.

Many believe that the sculptor adds shape and texture to the raw material to create the sculpture. That's one way of looking at it. I prefer to see the sculptor as simply removing from the raw material everything that isn't the sculpture. What remains IS the sculpture.

So where do we begin?

We begin with what cannot be argued: you are. You cannot say you are not. We start there.

That you are is a certainty. What you are is what we're trying to take a closer look at.

The underlying ground, the underlying essence is consciousness. When you look at people, when you look at mountains or oceans, when you do this you must be conscious.

You are conscious. You're conscious when you're asleep, you're conscious when you're awake. You can perceive objects, you can perceive movements and activities. When you dream, it's the same. It is within consciousness that all these images are projected. The consciousness that you are is what all the mental images appear on.

Once you realize that whatever appears to you cannot be you, you are free of all your personas and their demands. You clearly understand that the body is the proxy for the brain so that it can act in the world. Seeming individuals are survival machines, programmed to preserve and replicate the DNA.

You can watch the story knowing you are not the story.

Now, let's begin at the beginning of the story.

The male sperm fertilizes the female ovum. The consciousness latent therein takes over and the cell begins to divide. Organs develop, body develops, brain develops. Nine months later, there is birth.

As a baby, we don't yet have any sense of "I". There is no identification with a person. We are truly a transparent screen, on which phenomenon appear. We are as yet not influenced by the memes of our parents, teachers and peers and by the customs of the society in which we will grow up.

We simply are, in the absence of any labels, descriptions or definitions. Hunger, thirst, crying, eating, sleeping, just appear and disappear to us, on us. There is only awareness of whatever presents itself to us. We are pure openness without any divisions or ratings. There are no judgments, divisions, sortings, or projections. The standards imposed by culture, education or religion are not yet in place.

There is no reference point to whom all this happens; no decider or thinker or doer. There is only observing, absent any me and others, absent any past or future................ and most relevant, absent any problems. No lines of demarcation have been established, no points of beginning and ending. No sex, no nationality or identity. In fact, not even awareness of a body; in the purest sense, nobody.

All there is is the functioning: the processes of breathing, digesting, eliminating, growing, perceiving etc.

Then, at a time usually between 18 and 24 months, a new process is initiated: self consciousness. We become self-aware. There is "me" and "other than me", the birth of duality. All the pure data input, the registration of everything, is now filtered by the brain as it seeks to insure, firstly, survival, and second, reproduction.

It assigns relevance to all incoming data. altering, modifying and making projections from the data based on its expectations. Whatever is deemed not relevant to my survival and reproduction is not likely to be reflected in the brain's output.

We become aware of a voice, not a voice that is heard through the ears, but a voice that seems to originate somewhere in the head. The conventional term for this voice is mind. Rather than introduce this additional concept, I believe it is better to merely reference it as brain-speak. That is what it really is. It is a series of soliloquies primarily pertaining, once again, to the past, to the future, toward survival and reproduction. The balance is chatter, relatively unimportant.

To prove this to yourself, try to recall as many soliloquies from yesterday as possible. I suspect that, at best, the number will be in single digits. Yet, this brain-speak was going on every moment for the 16 or so hours that you were awake yesterday. If they have not been stored in memory, clearly the brain itself doesn't view them to be important.

As we grow, all sorts of memes or programs activate. Some are related to survival and reproduction of the species; others are installed by our parents, teachers and society as a whole in order for this so-called individual to develop into what is deemed functional.

Earliest on, parents reinforce that the name equals the body. Before that, we talk about ourselves in the third person sense. Therefore, the birth of the body precedes the birth of the person by about two years.

Of course, over time, this "me" becomes integrated.

The openness we experienced as a newborn is gone. In its place is the prison of a mind in a body. All attempts at improving the body or the mind are nothing more than the desire to make the prison more comfortable.

All the bodily sensations, all the feelings, all the thoughts and emotions become ours. Boundaries are set up; qualities are assigned. I am good, I am bad, I am this, I am that. Our experiences are all logged. The sum of all these is woven into a narrative, the story of me, my story. The brain is hard wired for this narrative, that is to say that it is inherent in its essential function.

The self conscious, the first thought, I am, expands outward encompassing more and more characteristics.

We are also told that this story must be a noble one, that we must achieve, that we must accomplish, that we must fulfill our purpose here, whatever that might be and however that could possibly be discerned.

That which used to be merely spontaneous is now believed to have been activated by one's own agency. We believe we have free will to choose what we do. We've been told that we can choose, that we can decide to do things or not to do certain things. We are now actors in the world.

All the brain-speak serves to confirm this and what others have said to us. We buy into it, all this hearsay, without ever checking.

But if it were really so, if we really controlled our lives, why are we not happy? Why are we searching outside ourselves to "make" us happy? Shouldn't we just be able to will a happy life?

Similarly, why do we feel isolated, afraid? Why are we unable to consistently make things the way we want them to be?

This is where we find ourselves, looking for someone, some thing, to provide a way out.

As is always the case when one is feeling lost, the way out is to go back the way one came.

Being

There is the Potentiality, in which nothing is other than primal awareness.

What is referred to as deep sleep is the first step toward actualization of the potential. It is content free, absent all percepts and concepts. There is no experience of deep sleep because there are no objects of experience. However, the absence of objects must not be taken to suggest the absence of consciousness.

In what we call dreaming, there is consciousness of content in the form of thoughts and images that come through the brain. We refer to it as the dream world.

In waking, there likewise is consciousness of the content. But now, the content additionally comes through the senses, requiring time and space. Therefore, an instrument in time and space, the body, is required. As such, the body and its world rise and set together. If the body does not rise again, meaning death, its world does not arise either. In both the dreaming and the waking states, there is manifestation, the actualization of the potentiality, Awareness. Consciousness is, as such, an aspect of awareness. It is the cognitive agency, the Subject.
*****

The Complex functions through all living objects.

In one case, it takes form as a cow. The cow grazes on grass and produces milk. It is being a cow, a cow-being.

In another case, its form is that of a tree. The Complex functions in it as roots shooting out to find moisture and nutrients in the soil. The branches and leaves evidence heliotropism, the tendency to turn towards the sun. When the cold season comes, the sap stops running and the leaves fall off. Spring comes; new buds and leaves form. Fruits and flowers appear, containing the seeds for new trees.

This is what it's like being a tree, a tree-being.

In yet another form, the Complex animates a human. It performs functions and actions too numerous to mention as a human-being. Sever the connection between the Complex and the object and the object dies. That rule is inviolate.

In that regard, all death is like an unplugged lamp. Absent a connection to the Complex, the object is inert, devoid of function and lifeless.

The above are three examples of being.

Yet, it is only in the last that we assign the concept of an entity to it; a person. We don't personify the cow, we don't personify the tree. Why is that.........and what is it that makes us so sure we're right about it?

The Echo of Being

Q: How do I know that what you are saying is the truth?
There is no stamp for the truth, no way to mark it. It is sufficient to determine whether or not what I am saying is false. The very nature of the false is to seem true.
Q: But I need to know.
Stop for one second and reflect. Haven't all your needs been met since that instant of your conception. Why should it be any different now? There's no reason to be preoccupied with needing to know.
Q: But, I feel as if I don't have a lot of time.
You need time to become; you don't need time to be. You are..................
a point of awareness, co-extensive with time and space. Individuality is merely the echo of Being. When the echo is gone, Being remains.
Q: In your talks, what you say sounds so passive. It almost sounds like you want me to vegetate.
That's hardly the case.
Everything that needs to happen will happen in the natural course of events. You go through it without resistance, facing tasks as they come, attentive and thorough. But the general attitude is of a subtle detachment, without expectation of defined outcomes.
Metaphorically, you walk on the ocean floor in the absence of turmoil instead of on the surface, battling the perfect storm du jour.
Q: You're indifferent.
No, I'm impartial. There are no preferences.
Q: That's where peace is found, right?
As long as we are seeking to find peace and happiness "somewhere," we are overlooking where peace and happiness are.
In the final analysis, that which is here doesn't recognize any "there".
Q: Why is all this the way it is?
All this is the way it is so that the world is as it is.
Nothing exists by itself; this is because that is .... and for anything to be, time and space are required. As such, time, space, the world and the you that are in it, come and go together.
Q: That's pretty heavy. Am I merely exchanging old concepts for new ones by listening to you?

This set of ideas or concepts is offered as a different way to make sense of your experiences. Every concept remains open to question. The only thing you cannot doubt is that sense of being which is prior to all concepts. I know that I am not a concept: I exist, that much I know. I can't say "I don't exist".

Despite all the changes to my body, to my thoughts, etc. during this lifetime, what has not changed is this ever-present energetic consciousness. It is the unchanging background against which a changing world appears, disappears and reappears.

Q: I like what you have to say. However, my life is really busy right now. Maybe I can begin to do this in sixty days or so. In that manner, I can gradually prepare for it.

Each moment is unique; no moment exists twice. Squander it and it is irretrievable.

All preparation is for the future; you cannot prepare for the present.

Q: It's now or never?

It's now or now. All there is is now.

Illusion

Just as seeing is the function of the eye, attention is the function of the brain. The function is already there before any object for the function appears. Once the object appears, it is cognized, named, and stored in memory. When it is seen again, it is re-cognized.

The entire process from perception through recognition happens in a split second. Then the brain refers the recognition to a fictional "central agent of recognition", the self or me. It creates a psychological representation of the original perception. This is a habituation that has been reinforced over millions of years and now is truly second nature. However, the brain is constantly making mistakes. Because of the tremendous amount of data coming in, the brain prioritizes processing speed over accuracy when creating a representation. Mistaking the psychological representation for the actual is the basis of illusion.

Our image of ourselves, our identity, changes over time. But that which supports the identity doesn't change. Every act of definition, of assigning labels to oneself, "I am this, I am that" further embellishes the illusion.

What is real is not imaginary, that is to say that it is not a product of the mind. Our moment-to-moment experience is filtered thru our minds; as such, it is not real. it is an illusion. Although one may balk at hearing this, one should ponder:

Which is the more successful illusion, the one that ends with an onstage bow and rabid applause, or the one that feels so real we never stop to think about it?

What binds that former identity to this me, and allows me to maintain the illusion that there is continuity from moment to moment and year to year? The element of continuity is entirely dependent on memory. The brain provides the glue that holds the seeming self together.

All there is is the interaction of the hardware and the software. There is no entity.

The brain is vulnerable and defenseless; it requires embodiment for its survival. Everything we perceive is processed by the brain in order to ascertain how the event/object relates to it. This is the fundamental structure of self and other, to allow the output to be coherent and organized. This is the translation of the self consciousness that has arisen in the body. Once all the internal properties of your nervous system are set, all the properties of your conscious experience, its subjective content and the way it feels to you, are mostly determined. The world appears to happen to us: that is all we can know about it. The entire world appears in you and not you in it. Representational models are created and revised in the brain. Events are coming and going in your presence. The brain bundles perception, cognition, and action in a way that selects just the right parameters for existing in the physical world from moment to moment.

There is some downside to this. For example, the brain is hardwired for pattern recognition. It finds patterns when they are there and it finds them where none exist.

In the final analysis, the brain is all about reactivity. It takes what is happening now and predicts what will happen next, and then sets the appropriate reaction.

What is Mind?

Q: What am I to do? I do not see myself as you see me. Maybe you are right and I am wrong, but how can I cease to be what I feel I am?

A CEO who believes that he is a clerk can be conclusively convinced in only one way: he must behave like a CEO and see what happens. Behave as if what I say is true and judge by what actually happens. Where's the downside risk? All I ask is the little faith needed for making the first step. With experience will come the confidence that is now absent.

Behave as if you were pure awareness, bodiless and mindless, space less and timeless, beyond 'where' and 'when' and 'how'. Dwell on it, think of it, learn to accept its reality. Don't oppose it and deny it all the time. Keep an open mind at least.

There is nothing to practice, per se. To know yourself, be yourself. To be yourself, stop imagining yourself as something particular.

Q: The sense of being a person persists.

The brain sustains the body, the Complex sustains the brain. Where is the person?

Q: In my mind.

You've taken the same problem and transferred it to another seeming thing.

What is the mind? The mind is not a thing. It's not an object; it's a function. Mind is what the brain does. It can be further broken down into these four sub-functions: memory, thought, reason and selfhood. So I'll repeat my question: where is the person?

Q: I can't give it a location, yet it still seems to be.

If you can't locate it yet it seems to be, can you concede that it might be an illusion?

Q: I think so.

That's a good starting point. Continue to come back to it. Every time you look for it and can't find it will reinforce the understanding of its illusory nature.

Q: You really just want me to give it up, don't you?

I don't suggest giving something up in order to obtain something better. Give something up when you have discerned it has no value.

Causation

Q: I have been meditating for fifteen years.
What have been the results?
Q: I have attained a certain degree of peace.
This peace you refer to isn't peace. It's fragile, destroyed by the smallest disturbance or inconvenience.
Q: I disagree.
No problem. Want to test it out?
Q: Sure
Work at a 7-11 for two weeks or spend that time with your in-laws. Then report back. (laughter).
Q: Not much I can say to that. But I was taught that meditating would bring peace to me.
True peace may arise; it may not. Don't confuse causation with correlation.
A raven sat on an apple tree and an apple fell. This does not create a casual relationship between the apple and the raven. You may attribute peacefulness to meditation, practices and effort. But when the apple fell, it fell on its own accord, not because of where the raven sat.
Once you create for yourself a world in time and space, governed by causality, you are bound to search for and find causes for everything. You may have heard me say that the world is uncaused. What do I mean by that?
Think of turning on a lamp. It is because the lamp, the wiring, the switch, the transformer, the transmission lines and the electricity form one whole, that you get the light. If any is lacking, the lamp doesn't light. Yet, I cannot single out any one of them as the cause.
For any event to occur requires the cooperation of the entire universe. Here's another example. Consider how many things had to align so that you could drive here today.
You had to remember to carry your car keys. Everyone in the oncoming traffic had to remain awake so as to not swerve into you. Your carburetor had to function properly. Your tires had to avoid puncture. I could go on.
However, I cannot say that your tires caused you to be here, nor your carburetor nor the other drivers nor your memory.

Everything is linked together; therefore everything has numberless causes. The entire universe contributes to the smallest thing. A thing is as it is, because the world is as it is.

My point is that when everything contributes to everything, the world itself is really without some singular cause. Any event is the product of numerous contributions. That's it.

Why get distracted seeking causes? Why do causes matter, when all appearances are transient? Let come what comes and let go what goes.

Hot Potato

Q: I'm sure that this will be a hot potato. Do we have free will or is everything predetermined?

To begin, I don't feel that the question is properly structured. That is to say that it presupposes that there is some "you" to have free will. Obviously, if there is no "you", the issue of "your" free will is moot. But let's not go up that slippery slope for now. Let's concede for the sake of this exchange that there is this "you" and we are trying to determine that it can choose as it wishes. OK?

Q: OK

The way I see it is that man indeed has will, but it is not free. That is to say that the will of man is dependent on the cooperation of the universe, the will of the universe, to coin yet another concept. Therefore, if your will is aligned with the will of the universe, you can do whatever you want to do.

Q: Here, look; I want to raise my hand and I raise it. That proves that I have free will.

No it doesn't. All that proves is that the universe was willing to cooperate in bringing this action to fruition.

You know, I only need to evidence the existence of a single black swan to invalidate the idea that all swans are white. In much the same way, positive outcomes don't confirm free will. However, negative outcomes disprove it.

So here goes: You want to be happy. I'm sure that's so. Why, then, aren't you happy every moment? It is your will to be happy, is it not?

Q: Sure it is.

So if you're not happy despite your will to be so, it means that you don't have the cooperation of the universe. The will of the universe trumps the will of the individual. That being the case, we cannot conclude that your will is free.

Q: What can we conclude?

What we can conclude is that we find ourselves between what has happened and what must happen and we tell ourselves we can do something about it.

The reality is that there is no difference between the movement of a wave in the ocean and the movement of the ocean. To speak of the wave's movement, independent of the ocean's movement, is ludicrous.

Similarly, there is also no difference between my actions and the actions of the Complex. To speak of any difference, is likewise ludicrous.

No Way

Q: I came here because a couple of friends of mine have worked with you and they claim to be very happy with the results. But to tell you the truth, I really don't have a good idea of what you do. They tried to explain it to me but it seemed to go over my head.

What I can say is that there definitely seems to be a change in them. I'm not sure if I can describe it. Maybe they just seem calmer and more at peace.

Anyway, could you tell me some more about your methods?

My sole interest is in directly ascertaining the truth of what-is from a starting point of complete neutrality.

I suggest that you accept no principle on faith alone, that you have no preconceived notions. We may know of the findings of others, but they do not taint our willingness to explore for ourselves.

We begin honestly from an admission of our conscious not-knowing, and inquire with an open mind in all possible ways, with the aim of finding the true nature of things for ourselves. We pursue this perfume much like a dog follows a scent, focused and unswervingly.

We begin now, which is the only time we have in which to do this.

We do not know what we expect to find other than to say that our objective is to find our definition, whatever the finding entails and wherever that finding takes us.

We have no map; we traverse no established territory. There is no way. All there is is a common beginning point: What is this I that is claimed as my own?

What ensues is an examination of how the external influences, regardless of source, regardless of form and intent, impact our view of things.

There is no formula, no "x" number of breathing exercises, plus "y" hours daily of chanting, plus "z" hours of meditation plus 10% of one's income, all for a period of 10 years equals Understanding.

No promises of attaining anything are extended; what you already are is not subject to attainment.

Q: I understand; you're not making any promises. But by the same token, nothing ventured, nothing gained; right?

You could phrase it that way. I would prefer to twist it around a bit: since nothing is lacking, nothing can be gained.

Just Suppose

Just because the world we perceive in waking appears to be more lasting and internally consistent than the world we perceive in dream, we cannot automatically conclude that it's more than a product of our imagination. Dreaming is a spontaneous process that creates a world out of the material springing forth from the mind. How does this differ from what we refer to as our waking state?

In the waking state, we return to where we left off, so to speak. Might this be because the waking state requires time, whereas dreams do not?

Q: Hold on one minute. Of course, dreams take place inside time.

They only take place inside time when viewed from outside the dream. Inside the dream, the images appear, one after the other giving a sense of continuity. But, we cannot determine how long any single image lasts.

Returning to where we left off, this bookmarking effect, doesn't negate the possibility that the two states are little more than imagination. There's another difference; when we're awake, there is a marked involvement with the protagonist and a lessened sense of witnessing the events that occur. This is the brain's way of acting in the world. Because its primary concern is survival, the brain treats this protagonist as itself.

I would argue that what we call waking state is closer to lucid dreaming. In a lucid dream, the dreamer can actively participate in and manipulate experiences in the dream. Lucid dreams seem real and vivid as do our more typical dreams.

Q: What I experience while awake seems more real.

You can't say that the waking state is more real because there's no such thing as more real. There's no pregnant and more pregnant. There's only real or not real. This is the mystery of imagination, that it all seems to be so real.

However, the matter is really quite murky. Clarify this for me if you will: last night, I was dreaming that I was a dolphin in the Pacific Ocean................... or was I a dolphin in the Pacific Ocean last night dreaming that I was Roy?

(pause)

We can't say with certainty, can we?

Out of deep sleep, a dream begins. Where was the dreamer before the dream began? The dreamer dreams the dream and then stops dreaming, returning either to wakefulness or to the state of deep sleep. Where has the dreamer gone?

(pause)

I hope I've made my point.

We know that about five waking hours per day are spent daydreaming, shifting attention away from some primary physical or mental task toward an unfolding sequence of private images or, more simply, "watching our own mental videos." Add to this the two hours per night that we dream.

As such, at the barest minimum, seven hours each day is nothing but imagination, and maybe it's a lot more than that. Let us examine what if it is a lot more?

Let's say that all our time waking and dreaming is dreaming. What can we say about the other 6 hours, while we are sleeping yet not dreaming? All we can say is "I don't know". Why do we say that? Because there was nothing there that was observable.

In that 6 hours period, there was the absence of all objects, of all perceivables. As such, we are aware of the absence. However, if the absence means absence of all objects, then there is no need for time and space during that period either. Now we're talking about another dimension altogether.

Q: I don't want to get more confused, so I'm asking what feels like a dumb question. What do you mean by real?

Actually, that's a very important question. Let's use God as an example, your God, as you choose to believe It to be.

If something is said to be real, then it exists. God is real means God exists.

God cannot exist one minute and not exist in the next. God always exists. That means that God always is. When we say "God is" we mean that God has being. "Always is" equals being which equals real. What comes and goes doesn't have true existence; it's temporal. It therefore lacks being and if it lacks being, it's not real. It's illusory.

From this, it's not much of a leap to hypothesize that anything subject to time is an illusion. But that's another matter for another day.

Perception

Light entering the eye triggers chemical reactions in the retina, these produce electro-chemical impulses which travel along nerve fibers to the brain. At this stage, there is only capture and recordation by the brain. But then the images are processed by the brain and are filtered for relevance, labeled and re-cognized.

I then have the experience of seeing a tree. But what I am actually experiencing is not the tree itself, only the image that appears in the mind. Consider the experience of the color green. In the physical world there is light of a certain frequency, but the light itself is not green. Nor are the electrical impulses that are transmitted from the eye to the brain. No color exists there. The green we see is a quality appearing in the mind in response to this frequency of light. It exists only as a subjective experience in the mind.

The same applies to our other senses as well.

As such, the world we perceive is always a filtration, an a priori distortion thru the prism of the brain.

Mystical Experiences

Q: I spent time with a mystic in India. He could describe in detail numerous out-of-body experiences that he had. How does that reconcile with what you're talking about or does it refute what you're saying?

The subjective image of our body emerges from the convergence of multiple senses, the balance system, and proprioception which is the sense of body position and movement.

The brain continuously checks and compares the sensory signals from the body with the motor signals, building a strong sense of embodiment, that is, of a self which is localized within one's bodily borders as if the body fits like a glove.

Out-of-body experiences can be elicited by electrical stimulation of the angular gyrus in the brain. As such, this kind of experience is not necessarily mystical, and is due to an electrical alteration in the normal embodiment process.

Q: Are you saying that the body having this conscious experience is of no value?

Everything has value; some things have more value than others. What often happens is that we overvalue an experience. There arises a great temptation to grasp it and keep it, to relive it or duplicate it.

Suddenly, we're off track. The grasping or duplicating becomes the task at hand rather than the seeing through all temporal experiences to the intemporal.

Too, the statement "a body having consciousness" is far less accurate than the statement "consciousness having a body".

Just as I am not the clothes that I wear, I am also not the body that I wear. However, I am aware of the body that I wear.

Q: But I remember certain spiritual experiences I've had. Should I just forget them?

A common error is mistaking dawn for high noon. You had an experience; now, it's done. If it was as life changing as you assert, then evidence the changes in your life.

Q: Yet, it felt like I had arrived, like I had reached my destination.

There are no experiences of the destination. All experience is on the way to the destination.

Q: Now it feels like you're trivializing it.

That's not my intention. I'm trying to counterbalance what feels to me like your placing an excessive value on the experience.

All experience is time bound. It comes, it goes, it leaves a residue as memory. But an experience and the memory of an experience are hardly the same. The recollection of the past is not the past. The past is a dead thing.

When does any recollection of the past occur? We re-collect the memory from the brain's data storage and bring it forward into here and now. We take now and here with us wherever we go. I am now here is the primal truth. In fact, NowHere is all there is.

On Death

Q: I'm attending here today to try to gain some insight on my fears surrounding death. Can you help me with that?

If any single idea is traumatic, it is the idea of death. This is because we are not able to disassociate ourselves from this identity with the body.

Q: I see no distinction between death and death of the body.

OK, but let's clarify things. You can't experience your death; you can only experience dying. Agreed?

Q: Sure.

What has happened is that you have reduced the totality, the limitless, to the limited: I am this body.

That is why, being unable to give up this association with the body, you are afraid of dying.

Q: That sounds great, but what do I do with that?

The investigation I speak about allows you to see more clearly that you are so much more than merely this body, which was born and which will die.

What I am talking about is not about who you believe you are but about what you really are. This discernment is the process of disillusionment, freeing yourself from illusion.

Q: How do I begin this investigation?

Ask yourself: "What is death?"

Death is the end of time, is it not? It is a returning to the time before time, to the timeless. It is a returning to the point of origin.

Q: Wasn't my point of origin at conception?

That's another way to begin the investigation. But, let's not digress. An antelope runs from a lion because it wants to continue living. This love of being is hard wired into the organism. As such, we mustn't equate the desire to live with the fear of death. There may be a fear of dying, of the experience being painful, etc.

However, we don't know death; we can only imagine death. We imagine it as the end of the Composite. So if there's fear, it's fear of the end of this persona.

It is the same thing as what holds people back from taking the hard look that I am speaking about. It puts the validity of the personal at risk.

Q: How do we overcome that aversion?

The willingness to see things differently is a good start.

The space inside a cup is dictated by the shape of the cup. Yet, when the cup is shattered, the space is unaffected. One could therefore argue that for the time that there is a body, the consciousness appears to be embodied.

In common parlance, we say that the eye sees. Yet, upon examination, we find that this is a misstatement. The eye is present in a cadaver. Yet, this eye cannot see. When the Complex abandons its host the body, the instrument of the eye cannot function. So it is the consciousness that sees, through the instrument of the eye.

Q: Where does the Complex go at death?

Where can it go? It is all-pervasive, everywhere. On the death of the organism, the consciousness goes on, unaffected.

When you are clear that you not limited to the Composite, then any fear of death loses its hold.

United States

During the course of a twenty four hour day, this psychosomatic organism experiences three different states or modes.

The first I will call the Default state. You know it as dreamless sleep. It comprises a full quarter of your day.

During this time, your senses are running on low power, so to speak. There is no awareness of the outside world. However, if the world intruded on you during this period, for example if someone threw a brick through your bedroom window, your senses would likely awaken you.

All your bodily functions continue. You don't perceive any images or thoughts, yet you remain conscious. You can say there was nothing there because you are conscious of their absence.

The next state might be called Maintenance state. It runs in ninety to one hundred twenty minute cycles. It is when REM or Rapid Eye Movement occurs and when images in the form of dreams typically appear.

The senses remain as before, on low, and the functioning of the body continues. There are no thoughts; you are conscious of their absence. However, images appear and disappear and they are observed. Approximately two hours each night is spent here.

The last of the three modes is the Fully Operational mode. It runs roughly sixteen hours in duration. All the senses are operating and the body functions as before. Perceptions, thoughts and sensations are all jockeying for senior position in consciousness. Most importantly, the thought "I am in this world" has arisen. One is now self conscious.

The point I would like to make is that you are none of these modes or states. You are that to which, the transparent screen on which, the discontinuous states appear and disappear. Being conscious is an experience recognized by you. Therefore, you must be prior to it.

The three are merely states of consciousness, supported by the Awareness that you are, the immovable center of all that moves. This Awareness is alive; it is Life itself. It is the intelligent energy that is the starting point and terminus of everything.

And you are That.

You know, in the final analysis, everything can be broken down into: That which is presently known and

The unknown, that which is yet to be made known.

However, what I am pointing to serves as the container for these. It can only be called the Unknowable. It is not anything in particular.

Therefore, not being a thing, it cannot be known.

The only way to know it, please excuse my taking this linguistic license, is to be it.

This is my invitation to you.

This usually prompts the response "Yes, Roy, but how to do it?"

How can I show you how to be what you are? Would it make any sense if I said "Don't be what you aren't"?

Rigor

You are perceiving. You didn't decide to perceive. It happened.
You are functioning. You didn't decide to function. It happened.
At the appropriate time, as part of that functioning, self consciousness arose. You didn't decide to become self conscious. It happened.
This arising is purposeful. Its purpose is protect the organism, to situate it vis-a-vis its environment. All living organisms, in order to continue living, must have access to information relevant to their survival. For example, a mouse that cannot sense the vicinity of a cat, or find its way to food or to a mate, is less likely to survive and to pass on its genes than the mouse that can.
This is the primary drive in humans too. The brain creates a frame of reference, a center of reference, for this. This reference is me. Then the life-long narrative ensues.
Yet, at no time was an entity created.
The thoughts that arise, the thoughts that are "heard" are brain-speak. My thoughts means thoughts referring back to me.
Millions of bits of data are assaulting the brain every second. The brain can only handle a small fraction. So it sorts them for relevance, with the center of reference being me. It then rejects what doesn't meet the standard and processes the balance. This creates a point of view that must be, by its very nature, fragmentary. We act as if we see the big picture, but this is self deception.
Q: You seem to be pretty rigorous about this. You don't provide us with much wiggle room.
If I allow people to continue to view themselves as they have, what have I done for them? I've allowed them to perpetuate the status quo. But if I show them how to see themselves as they are in reality, quantum change can occur.
What seems personal is only an appearance, much in the same way that a color needs a surface to appear on. Forms come and go; what they appear in is eternal. All phenomena come to you. Each serves as a reminder of your essential being, the fact that you are.
Please send me a text message when you aren't. (laughter)

Mind + Body or the Eternal Constant

Q: It often feels like my body and my mind are not in sync.
When you say "my body and my mind, what does "my" refer to?
Q: "My" refers back to me.
This me must be something different than the body and the mind that it claims as its own. What is it?
Q: It's the person that I am.
This person that you are, isn't the body and the mind part of that?
Q: Yes, I guess.
So we've completed the circle but haven't clarified who the body and mind belongs to.
(Silence)
I want to stress that this is more than semantics.
This combination of life force energy cum consciousness is what animates and sustains the body and its processes. Because the brain is hard wired for narrative, attention gravitates toward the story of a body-mind named Carol. Admittedly, the story can be engaging.
But fixating on the narrative misses the actuality.
That actuality is that you are the singular point of intersection of time and space where everything appears. The very Now, the very Here.
Q: How do I lighten the load?
Everything must be scrutinized and the unnecessary left behind.
Or, here's another way to look at it. You can do it in reverse. Start by believing you are this cognizing presence and then identify and eliminate anything that obscures it.
Q: I can't do that. The appearances distract me.
These appearances are a gift; they allow you to recognize your own changelessness against the foreground of change. Whatever appears, you are the Eternal Constant that was already present before it arrived.
The so-called person is objectively observable. Watch it, study it. Its mechanistic nature will become obvious and you will realize that you are so much more than the habitual.
Q: Yet, the habitual is deeply ingrained.
Yes, however, habits can be changed.......................and believing that there is a person inside is only a habit.
Behaving habitually takes no effort at all; the neural networks are all in place. A single stimuli arrives and off we go.

Q: I can't seem to muster up the resolve.

Imagine you're in a movie theater. You're enjoying the movie; it is engrossing, engaging. Suddenly, you feel pressure from your bladder. Should I get up and go to the toilet or should I stay? No, I'm enjoying the movie too much. I'll stay. Then the pressure increases, but you decide to tough it out. There may come a time when the urge to urinate becomes greater than the urge to stay involved with the movie. When that happens, you turn your attention away from the movie, you get up and you attend to what requires attending.

It's the same thing here. When the urge to disentangle yourself from this egocentric viewpoint is sufficiently strong, you have the ability to turn your attention away from the movie, get up and attend to what requires attending.

Conflict

Peace that is merely the intermission between two conflicts is not peace.
True peace exists only when the one who needs peace is no longer
there. As long as you exist as someone who seeks peace, you've created
conflict. To be a human being is the very essence of conflict.

Darwinism or the survival of the fittest has no regard for the future. Its
sole imperative is to gain an advantage over others in the species so that
it may continue and replicate. Conflict is inherent in this.

Too, we are psychologically set up for conflict. What do we fear most?
We fear our own absence, the end of me. What do we long for most?
We long for peace, our own absence, the end of this oppressive me.
So we have the pushing away from absence while pulling toward
absence at the same time. Could I possibly describe a better prescription
for conflict?

When we are unwilling to accept life on its terms, when we want things
to be different from what they are, when we define ourselves by our
preferences, all of these sow the seeds of conflict.

Q: OK, so what do we have to do to step out of it?

You step out of it by refusing to step in to it.

To be conscious of self consciousness is the movement away from
individuality.

This life, this me in the world, is a singular event extended in space and
time and perceived in consciousness. There is no individual; PERIOD.
We don't make any effort to acquire this identity. Nor do we have the
intention to acquire one. It simply arrives; it appears.

The recognition of appearance as appearance takes you out of it.
Overlooking the obvious, oh-so simple truth is the only impediment.
No breakthroughs or goings-beyond are called for.

During this thought, after this thought ends, and before the next
thought appears, I have been and continue to be.

Q: There's nothing to do?

When something favorable happens to us, we attribute it to Grace. If
the event is unfavorable, we resign ourselves to its being God's will.
Either way, the "I" did nothing.

Does life stop while you are trying to decide what to do next? You may
have stopped thinking but you're still aware. This instant takes you
beyond thought. There is no reason to be concerned about what to do.

Doing will happen on its own when the need arises. What needs to be done gets done. Stop worrying about it and return to alertness.

Q: Are you saying that I just have to concentrate on being alert?

No, I'm not.

Concentration is always on the particular whereas alertness is global. It is not a form of hyper-vigilance. Being open and receptive to whatever comes, being welcoming, is being alert.

Q: The end result is the end of all conflict?

There may continue to be opposites, but in the same manner as Winter is not in conflict with the Summer, there is no opposition.

The Mechanics of Being Mechanical

Q: Taking your advice, I have tried to set some time aside to look at myself in a fresh light. What I have discovered is a bit disturbing. The degree to which I do the same things over and over, the degree to which I respond in what seems to be a very mechanical manner, bothers me.

I would like to suggest that you cut yourself some slack.

Strictly speaking, one cannot help being habitual and mechanistic. Our bodies are programmed by Nature and most of our mental and emotional processes are directly tied in with this, however individualistic and spontaneous the processes may seem to us. More forms of conditioning are sourced by our societies and cultures.

Our moods, values, desires, fears, perceptions, and reactions are largely derived from this software.

The goal, therefore, is not improvement of the programming. We are not seeking to upgrade the software; that would mean only making one to be a happier or more peaceful automaton.

The goal is the transcendence of the software, to no longer be a machine. It is achieved through de-education and self confrontation.

Q: I assume that what you mean by self confrontation is this examination process that is presently underway. But, what do you mean by de-education?

At its simplest, de-education means the release of the known. That is to say that it is a setting aside of what we think we know, all that we have learned, all that we have been told that we have taken to be true, all our opinions and ideas about the way things ought to be.

It is tabula rosa, the blank slate. Onto it, we can write our findings from the examination that is ongoing without polluting the examination with our inherent biases.

Q: What I'm finding is this: In so many ways, I am like a computer. Unless I am plugged in, so to speak, the unit cannot operate; it is, in fact, dead. Therefore, the unit, be it a computer or a person, requires a source of energy to sustain it. I'll call that source God, although other names would be equally applicable.

Go on.

Q: In each and every moment, the hardware, or soma, receives the input from the environment. It is processed by the software, or psyche, which provides the output, that is, the reaction. This is the fruit, to date, from what I've been working on.

How do you feel about what you've discovered?

Q: As I said before, I find it disturbing. Yet, curiously, at the same time, it is sort of exhilarating in that I feel I have peeled away a small fragment of what has been covering what really is.

I would say that you're definitely on the right track. I don't want to say any more without setting up an expected outcome, some picture of what you are supposed to find. Suffice it to say, keep up the good work.

Preliminary Investigations

The brain sustains the functioning of the body. But what sustains the brain?

All experience, sensation, perceptions and conceptions, is the knowing of the output of the brain. What is it that is conscious of this output? You're not the same person you were ten years ago or even ten seconds ago. Your chemistry has changed, your cells have changed, your blood has moved around, your thoughts have changed. And "your mind" is full of thoughts and ideas from "other minds," and all of us are breathing in and out, exchanging air and chemicals and subatomic particles and thoughts and vibrations of one kind or another.

Where are the boundaries?

The Futility of the Search

Q: Why do you say that all searching is futile?

Searching is futile so long as the searching is for some object. The answer to your questions, the end of the search, does not reside in any object. It is found in the subjective and this cannot be perceived.

Q: So I am only wasting my time?

For me to say that you are wasting your time would be a judgment on my part. I can say that you are spending your time. You can decide whether or not it is time well spent.

Q: I think the time was well spent. I know that I've made progress.

Toward what?

Q: Toward becoming more peaceful, toward becoming clearer about things.

Yes, all searching is about becoming something that you are not now. It is about attaining something that you believe is absent now. But is it so?

Q: What do you mean?

As I said, all searching is about trying to find what you believe is absent, whether that absence relates to a personal quality, a way of being, or whatever.

I would argue that what you believe is absent really isn't absent at all. It is only obscured. Remove the obscuration and what you thought was absent will be seen to be shining right there within you.

Q: How do I do that?

The nature of attention is to focus in on one thing at the expense of other things.

For example, if I write the word "dog" on this blackboard and I ask you what you see, your likely response will be to say "I see the word dog" whereas the more complete answer would be "I see the word dog on the blackboard". In this example, the blackboard has been lost, so to speak.

What you believe to be absent is equivalent to the blackboard in my example.

Q: Maybe so, but you haven't answered my question.

(laughing) You're right; I haven't.

What could I do to make you see the blackboard other than to call your attention back to it? I am inviting you to check out whether what you believe to be absent is really absent. But I can't check it out for you.

Q: I want to understand you; I really do. But I'm not sure that it is happening.

Can you see the subtlety of all this? Now you are searching for understanding!

The Scientific View

All the cells in the body are replaced within seven years. This body that you presently claim to be yours didn't exist seven years ago. Where is that body from seven years ago now? How many bodies can be called yours?

If I replace every single part of the Apollo 11 Space Shuttle, can I rightly refer to it as Apollo 11?

Science admits that the body is 99.99% empty space. It appears to be solid, but it isn't.

Likewise, the sky appears to be blue, but it isn't. The ocean also appears to be blue, but it too isn't. The sun appears to rise and set, but it doesn't. The earth we stand on appears to be still, but it's actually moving faster than 100,000 kilometers per hour.

We simply cannot equate appearance with actuality.

In the old scientific paradigm, your consciousness is regarded as an epiphenomenon of your brain, that is to say that the brain comes first, then consciousness. However, this theory has pretty much been refuted.

In the new paradigm, consciousness is the ground of being and your brain is the epiphenomenon.

In turn, the hardware of the brain runs the software that is called the mind.

In the 1970s, Benjamin Libet was involved in research into neural activity in the brain. His work soon crossed into an investigation into human consciousness.

One of his significant findings was that a person's brain seems to commit to certain decisions before the person becomes aware of having made them.

Most recently, researchers recorded mounting brain activity related to a resultant action as many as seven seconds before subjects reported the first awareness of the conscious will to act. These same researchers were then able to predict whether subjects would press a button with their left or right hand up to 10 seconds before the subject became aware of having made that choice.

The clear implication of this is that the concept of free will, of an entity with independent agency, is an illusion.

Like the reflected image in a mirror, you can argue that it really is, you can argue that it really isn't. But what can asserted with certainty is that it appears to be.

It is acknowledged that a lot of human behavior is genetically preset. All life forms are set up to be what they genetically express, and we must agree that a lot of who we are as human beings is predetermined by our genes.

Therein, the brain has a default setting that work against us. This setting is that we want to believe, we are programmed to find patterns and believe. Within that context, it is easy for us to believe that we have free will.

However, Libet's work and the work of others is a clear call to have a closer look.

Clarifying Me

Q: I've been trying to follow along, but when you said that there is no me, you lost me, pardon the pun.

There is nothing more sacred to the human personality than the sense of being a separate person with a life that has meaning. But this is only a belief ingrained since around the age 2 and is not the truth of what actually is.

There is a very subtle point here that I want to again revisit for clarification.

I've been yelled at for speaking in this manner. I've had objects hurled at me. People have a real emotional charge surrounding this.

When I say that there is no me, I am talking about the absence of an entity, some being that decides to initiate the actions undertaken by the body.

In the strictest sense, there is, in fact, a me. The me that exists is the sum of all the brain processes that are ongoing in the pursuit of survival of the organism.

To just go running around declaring, "There is no me, there is no me" misses this subtlety. There is a me, but there is no entity functioning as such.

Q: Then, as you see it, what is the me that I'm referring to?

The me that you're referring to is agent and owner. It is owner in so far as everything points back to my this and my that. It is agent in so far as everything points back to I plus some action; I think, I drive, I eat, etc. But when you make statements like "I digest" or "I urinate", the hollowness of this supposed agency is revealed.

Q: If I don't digest or urinate, who does?

"What does?" would be more accurate.

That which beats your heart, which replaces your cells, which heals wounds, That does…… and this That cannot be described as it resides outside perception and stands outside of space and time.

When words fall away, what's left to be said?

Q: Why can't I get past this me seeming to be real?

Because you are mesmerized by it. I refer to it as Entity Trance.

It seems so real, it seems so close to you that in fact, you assume it must be real. But as you step back from it, the perspective changes in the same way as the closer you stand to a huge billboard, the less you see and the farther from it you stand, the more that is revealed.

Q: I think I'm catching on. The more distance that I can create, the more accurate the view.

Well said. Can I use that or do you plan to copyright it? (laughter)

Experience

Consciousness is the observing of the ecology of the organism, i.e., via the senses as perceptions, via the bodily sensations as feelings and via thought/imagination as conceptions. It is the experiencing of these energies on the porous screen which everything appears on and passes through.

In that sense, consciousness is the Primary Experience.

So-called personal experience is merely this consciousness filtered through the neurology of the organism, the result being self-consciousness.

Therefore, the experiences we talk about are merely our own inner mental states. What's "out there" is dependent on what's "in here" or, stated in another way, experience is the interaction between what's "out there" and what's "in here".

Searching for the boundary between the experiencer and the experienced presumes that both have limits; one ends "somewhere" and the other begins "somewhere else". However, with thorough investigation, what is seen is that both of these are contained in, and are therefore aspects of, experiencing.

Control

Q: As time passes, my unhappiness gets bigger and bigger. I seem to have less and less control over my life.

That makes perfect sense.

At the root of all unhappiness is the inability to control circumstances and situations. It is the reluctance to accept the way things are in the moment.

Look at what can't be controlled:

Thoughts

Feelings

Sensations

Body functions

Actions

The unwillingness to accept the inability to control manifests as resistance. However, resistance only extends the duration and intensity of the discomfort.

Q: Are you suggesting that I need to accept the way things are even if I find them to be unacceptable?

Life is an ongoing oscillation between the preferred and the not preferred. The oscillation can only end when preferences end. Then life is a steady state of peace.

Q: I don't buy that.

I'm not trying to sell it. For that matter, I'm not trying to sell you on anything. What I am suggesting is that you check it out yourself.

For how long can you control the thoughts that appear? If you had any control at all over them, you'd only think happy thoughts, wouldn't you?

Same goes for feelings; would you ever choose to feel sad?

Q: Well, maybe not. But I know that I control my actions.

So it would seem. Yet, consider this: a moment ago you scratched your face. If you control your actions, you could tell me how you did that. Can you? If you can't tell me how you did it, that calls into question whether or not you did it at all.

Q: Now I'm starting to feel lost.

Don't confuse being lost with being in unfamiliar territory.

I realize that I am suggesting that you examine assumptions that you previously consider inviolate. That's OK.

The way out, so to speak, is to retrace the way you came. That means taking a look at these core assumptions and seeing whether or not they are true. If you find them to be true, keep them. Otherwise, it's time to let them go.

It's the letting go of what is seen to be untrue that opens the door to where you say you want to go.

So, accept my invitation and see. What you want may not be as far away as it seems.

Believing is Seeing

The first time I got really clear that there were instances that what I was seeing was what I was expecting to see was one day I was walking down the street and a man on a motorcycle stopped in the crosswalk, waiting for the traffic light to change.

He was wearing a black leather jacket and gloves, big boots and other items that would be considered normal biker fashion. My first quick look at him revealed his long hair flowing out from the back of his jacket. Yet, on closer scrutiny, I was shocked to see that he didn't have long hair at all. What I subsequently saw was a dark colored scarf flowing out from the top of his collar.

There's a part of each of us that doesn't want to question, doesn't want to inquire and verify. We'd prefer to believe what we expect and to expect what we believe.

Take a look at the image of a duck I'm projecting onto the wall. It's pretty straightforward, right? I'll turn off the projector now.

In this example, the familiar form you see causes your brain to recognize a pattern in the shape of some type of bird. The temporal lobes, which are the brain's center for decoding and recognizing patterns and objects, lock into a memory. The picture activates a few hundred million neurological circuits, which fire in a unique sequence throughout specific parts of your brain, and you are reminded of a duck. The memory imprinted in your brain cells of what a duck looks like matches the picture before you. This enables you to recall the word "duck." This is how we interpret reality, as a pattern recognition.

Now let's get outrageous for a moment.

What if I told you that you were mistaken, that you didn't see a duck? What if I told you that what you saw was a rabbit instead?

Let's look at the image again [projector on]. In an instant, your brain reorganizes its circuitry to imagine a rabbit instead of a duck. The brain has the ability to make adjustments to what it was expecting and fire in new combinations of patterns.

Can you see the subtlety of all this. In the beginning, I told your brain what to expect. My exact words were "look at the image of a duck". You saw a duck. Then I said "Oops, it isn't a duck; it's a rabbit". Now, you see a rabbit.

The point of all this is to highlight that when you are no longer processing information with a bias toward what the outcome will look like, you can see the world, and see yourself, differently.

The Only Question

Q: I have so many questions. Where should we begin?

There may be endless legitimate philosophical and religious questions plaguing you. Yet they all have as their common denominator your skewed self definition and therefore your skewed vantage point on existence. It is best to put all these secondary questions aside and work instead on answering the critical one. This will resolve all the other ones as well.

This requires the total, direct, naked confrontation of oneself in this very moment, apart from all of one's beliefs, imaginings, ego-indulgences, and projections, and focusing all of one's attention on the only salient question: "What is this I that everything relates to?"

This is possibly the most difficult and critical undertaking in all of life. It threatens to negate all that we know, have, and are. Therefore, it makes good sense that one encounters tremendous resistance to this inquiry and that numerous strategies, both overt and covert, may arise to forestall the process.

Q: You do make it sound scary.

To this structure, this seeming person, it can be quite scary. I mean............ we're talking about the end of its mastery over you. It's the end of decades of charade. That ain't small potatoes.

Facing the end of its reign of terror, I wouldn't expect this character to react in any other way than to try to put this off.

However, I can say to you that in all likelihood, the character doesn't dissolve; it will continue. What will end is the trance-like grip that holds over you.

Q: What does that leave, then?

It leaves freedom from the sway of the personality, freedom from the seemingly unending storyline that's been perpetuated.

Q: Can I think about it and get back to you?

Of course you can. But recognize that you've created the first in what may very well be a litany of justifications for postponement.

Q: But I can always begin at a later date.

Yes you can. But telling yourself this is a violation of the Eleventh Commandment.

Q: The Eleventh Commandment? What's that?

Thou shalt not fool thyself.

A Thought or Two About Thinking

We don't control our thoughts; they merely appear. There is no thinker nor is there a site in the brain where thoughts are produced. There are however, sites in the brain where thoughts are processed.

The thought is a vertical movement. However, thinking is horizontal, stretched out over time. So, if a thought appears and there is no attachment to it, it bursts like a bubble. Then, a subsequent thought appears.

Thinking is the attachment to a thought. We extend it.

That having been said, there are two types of thinking. The first is functional thinking. This refers to completing a task, balancing the checkbook or building a model airplane. It occurs in the present and incorporates total attention. During that time, there is complete involvement yet, in a sense, there is no "you".

The other form of thinking is the fixation on the past and/or projection of an imagined future. It is totally concerned with the perpetuation/fulfillment of the organism. "You" are totally involved with it.

The breaking of this trance-like hold is all that I speak about.

Intellectual Understanding

Is what I'm saying making sense to you?

Q: To tell you the truth, when I first started working with you, it was difficult for me because a lot of what you were saying didn't match with the way I was looking at things. But now that we've been at it this short while, I would answer with a "yes"; things are making sense. Yet, there's still this problem. I mean, I have the intellectual understanding but it doesn't seem to have filtered down to where it needs to go. Do you understand what I mean?

Let's stop right here!

If I tell you that you are a woman, do you need to have an intellectual understanding of that, or do you just know it?

Q: I just know it.

Well, it's the same for what I have been pointing to.

When you say you have an intellectual understanding, you haven't gotten it yet. That's because this is not to be understood intellectually. Instead, this is a deep knowing, something that does not have to look to the intellect for affirmation.

Q: OK, so what do I need to do to get this deep knowing?

What did you need to do to get to know that you are a woman? It's the same thing.

Q: Then there's nothing I can do?

I'll tell you what you will do. You'll react. A stimulus will appear and there will be a reaction to it. That's what the organism does. Then another stimulus and another reaction; and so on. The sum of all the inputs is Life and all the corresponding outputs are "you".

Yet, behind all this activity is an observing of all the activity. It is this observation that is your essential core. What I refer to as the core assumption is that you believe that you are an entity, a person, whereas direct investigation invariably reveals that you are the observing of the story, of the entity, of the person.

Q: That does clarify it for me.

Good, then what are you going to do now?

Q: That's a trick question. As the observing, all I can do is observe. As the organism, all I can do is react.

Well done.

Practice

Q: Recently, I went up into the mountains and just sat. After I time, everything became quiet and I had an experience of the oneness you refer to.

Then it will sadden you to be told that you simply can't have an experience of oneness. An experience of oneness requires both that which is experienced and the one that experiences. By my math, that makes two.

However, the two can resolve into experiencing, which is the oneness where there is no one experiencing.

Q: But if I can't experience oneness, what are all these practices for?

In spiritual circles, there is a lot of talk about one's practice, the nature of the practice, the amount of time allotted for the practice, etc.

However, I have yet to find anyone who has been freed due to their practice. Even the Buddha was not freed by practice. In fact, it wasn't until he rejected all practices that his enlightenment arrived.

If the practice cannot free me, what's the point of practice? Might the point be that there is nothing that one can do to become what one already is?

Q: I don't agree. There are millions of people all over the world who practice on a daily basis, some for hours each day.

Where is the so-called attainment that they have to show for it? Practices deny what is already present; they are about becoming something that you believe you presently aren't.

Practices can't take you to a place you've never left. Although I'll concede that it may seem as if you've left, I'm suggesting that you double-check.

Q: To you, then, even yoga is a waste of time; am I right?

I am not anti-yoga. It, too, has a place.

My concern with yoga, that is, the integration or unity of the body with the mind, is that it still leaves you believing that you are a body with a mind.

What Am I?

What do I seem to be?

My body as a composite entity.

My specific body sensations.

My personality, attitudes, desires, ego, feelings, reactions; all of that which comprises the person.

My mental processes, all the values, judgments, beliefs, evaluations that constitute the mind.

My assorted social and functional roles throughout the day (spouse, parent, child, employee, athlete).

My more consistently maintained roles (white, Anglo-Saxon Protestant, British, man/woman).

My identification with possessions or projections (my car, my mate, my appearance, my opinions).

My identification with my circumstances, events, interpersonal relationships, history………. in sum comprising the "story"

My mental experience of observation, discernment, and awareness

My physical experience of events happening

However, these are all observable and, as such, cannot be what I am.

The true point of reference is the very experience of subjectivity. It is the neutral screen on which everything appears and disappears. It is what uses the body as its instrument. It is what drops the body at death. It is Being; it is experienced thru the mind first as "I", then "I am", then "I am this or that". It is thru the mind that two confusions arise.

The first is owning, the idea of my thoughts, my body. The second is acting, what I do, did, or will do. When both are clearly seen thru, what is revealed is that they point back to their point of origin, the conscious agency which is both the owner and the actor.

It seems as if the world happens to a person, but in fact, there is only the perceiving of the world. When the perception goes thru the prism of the mind, the world seems to happen to the person.

Limitations of Insight

At its most basic, the sense or notion of "me" is a survival mechanism, activated at the time the infant became self conscious.

The data we select from our total experience is filtered primarily for its relevance to our survival. Next, it is filtered relative to our immediate needs; lastly, to reproduction of our DNA.

We look for nourishment, lovers, friends, social status, and security. Therefore, this type of sorting must divide our sensory input into two categories: that which can be used to support survival and that which can be discarded.

The usable data, despite being the smaller of the two sets, is taken in and processed, while the vast majority of the information is ignored, implicitly rejected. On one level, this type of management information system is quite effective as a survival strategy. However, the cost, so to speak, is that it places a strict limitation on our sensitivity and perception.

Q: Yes, but without survival, nothing else matters.

Of course; however, this is a type of black and white thinking that doesn't serve us.

You see, we also use this management system to inflate and sustain our ego needs. We are constantly seeking out confirmation of our opinions and beliefs. What provides this is taken in and embraced. Behavioral scientists refer to this as confirmation bias.

What challenges or denies our picture of ourselves is rejected. This selectivity operates on all levels from the overt to the covert.

Q: I still don't see anything wrong with that.

I'm not trying to say that it's wrong. I am only calling to your attention that it is limiting.

If we could suspend this constant scanning, if we could bring about a cessation of all these filters, there is then the opportunity for something greater to arise.

Q: What might that be?

It is the recognition of a presence, an aware energy that permeates every aspect of life. Over the centuries, ancient seers gave it many different names. But the name is not the thing, regardless of what the name may evoke in you. The word "water" cannot quench thirst nor can the word "chocolate" satisfy a sugar craving.

So I won't name it.

Q: Then what can you say about it?

Unperceived, it causes perception. Unfelt, it causes feeling. Unthinkable, it causes thought. Non-being, it gives birth to being. It is the immovable background of all motion. Whatever I say about it will be inadequate. All attempts to describe the indescribable must fail. Therefore, it must suffice to refer to it as the Ineffable

Q: So, where are we?

We are awash in It, we are afloat in It. It is what carries us, what sustain us. It is closer to us than our own eyes, yet most are blind to It. It is our very essence and to miss It is to miss everything.

Q: Now, I'm feeling a bit lost.

Don't try to figure it out. Allow my words to sink in; your inner compass will turn to True North. The rest will take care of itself.

Inattention

Q: You and I appear to be quite different.

The differences are only notional. Suppose two people look at a tree. One sees the bird twittering among the leaves and the other does not. Otherwise there is no difference. The one that sees knows that with a little attention the other will also see.

What you take yourself to be is merely the result of inattention. Direct your gaze through yourself to before yourself. You are where you are because of the way in which you think. Change the way you think and change the way you are.

Q: What do you mean?

Thoughts, emotions and feelings can begin and end. But that onto which the thoughts appear has no beginning or end. Let them all come, let them all go. Don't assign labels to them or have any preferences. In this way, the flow of energy is not restricted. You will find that sometimes the sky is cloudy and the sun seems to be covered. Sometimes it is clear. In either event, so what?

Q: So what? I don't get it.

If the self-reference point is seen to be insubstantial, it will be understood that whatever mental concept or image comes up naturally happens by itself. There's no need to get rid of it. It has purpose.

It can be useful for the assistance or defense of the organism, like changing colors comes about for an animal or bird. There's no thinking about protection; a natural camouflage occurs, without any conscious effort or trying to change the appearance. With or without belief in an independent entity, action comes about naturally to suit whatever situation arises.

Q: How then do I live my life?

Did you know how to live it before this question arose, or did it simply unfold before you? Don't seek understanding about this. It is better just to avoid misunderstanding.

Q: But I'm faced with many problems. What do I do about them?

Your troubles are all imaginary. The only cause of the problems, questions, doubts and issues in life is identifying with an appearance, this Composite of the body, the mind and all the narrative about them. You are not a thing which is perceived, but perception itself.

Q: I don't agree.

That's fine with me.

My contention is that the person merely appears to be, like the space within the bottle appears to have the shape and volume of the bottle. I'm suggesting that you check it out; maybe you'll change your mind.

Some Misunderstandings

The person is not the experiencer; the person is just another thing or event that is experienced. No person has a story; the person IS the story. We don't enter the world with any ideas or thoughts. It's virtually all acquired. We pick it up at a later time, yet we assume it's been there all along.

Your world is personal to you. I don't see everything you see; I don't hear everything you hear. I don't have the same thoughts nor do I have the same point of view. Even the experiences we tell ourselves we share aren't the same. In one case, they've been filtered through you; in the other, they're filtered through me. In each case, the outputs are vastly distinct.

If we can admit that what we are seeking is indescribable, how do we go about seeking it? And how do we know if we've found it? If God or Tao or Consciousness or whatever is everywhere, the notion of searching for It seems fairly ridiculous, doesn't it?

Atheism

Q: I've listened to you for a while now and one of the things that strikes me is that you don't make reference to God. Are you pushing atheism? Do you believe in God?

You see, the word God has a lot of different concepts for a lot of different people. With some, it is Christ, and with others it is Buddha, and with others it is something else.

If my god is not your god, to you my god will be, at best, a lesser god and at worst, irrelevant. Therefore, I'm going to take a bit of license here. When you ask if I believe in God, I will take that to mean what you're really asking is if I believe in your God.

Now, if I were, let's just say, a Hindu, I wouldn't believe in Jesus. So, if Jesus is your god of choice, so to speak, then to you I'm an atheist. Make sense?

Q: Sure.

OK, let's expand on that.

Likewise, I'm an atheist to Buddhists, Muslims, Taoists, and Jews; all told, I'm an atheist to about 2/3s of all the people on the planet.

My point, then, is that we're really all atheists. The only difference is that the list of gods I don't believe in may have one name on it more than yours.

Q: I never looked at it quite like that before.

Asking you to reconsider your point of view is what these exchanges are all about.

Q: Then you have no belief in a supreme being?

I believe that there is an Organizing Principle to everything. It is an intelligent energy that, as manifestation, is everything. Whatever is the fundamental source of creation, it itself must be without beginning, uncreated. Otherwise, there is a hidden creator lurking in the background, and then we must ask who or what created that.

It, itself, has no attributes; as such, it evades description.

It is eternal, existing outside space and time. It was there before there was "there" and "before".

It has no agenda, nor does It have preferences. It doesn't side with one football team over another. (laughter)

Q: Does this mean that the rabbis, the priests and the monks don't fulfill some purpose?

Sure they do. Their respective religions have appointed them to be intermediaries. They all belong to the Union of Middlemen for God. (laughter)

Unless God has some sort of speech impediment, where is the need for middlemen?

Q: Are you suggesting that worship is a waste of time?

Not at all.

Worship as God that which arrived with you; this life force and this consciousness together. That is the only God anyone can know; any other God is only something you've created.

Therefore, pray to the force in you that created the concept of God. Worship the power, the intelligent energy which sustains your very existence.

Let this be your God.

Q: And what about prayer?

What prayer can there be other than one that is seeking to overrule or influence God's Will? Unconditional acceptance of God's Will eliminates the need for prayer.

Q: Is there any place for sin and virtue in your view?

All sin and virtue is personal, much of which is dictated by the standards of one's society. Within the context of the impersonal, sin and virtue are nonexistent.

Q: To sum it up then, you are against religion?

I'm not for or against anything. I would simply call your attention to that which divides and that which unites, that which includes and that which excludes.

If you feel that religion has a place in your life, that's fine with me. If you choose to believe in God, then acknowledge that all is God's and all is for the best. Welcome all that comes with acceptance and thankfulness.

However, it's important for you to remember that every exclusion, every division, is a movement away from the unity we've been talking about here over these many weeks.

Getting Centered

Q: Before I came here, I took a few minutes and centered myself. Yet, somehow, I'm not feeling very centered.

My suspicion is that this is because the centeredness you sought was only a centering of the small self, the self derived from the arising of self consciousness. As such, it is quite fragile.

The small self will undoubtedly feel threatened and anxious by my words.

The whole notion of centering is just another story we weave. What you truly are, as I have been trying to drive home, is this Complex of consciousness plus the energy or life force that sustains everything. It is Life itself.

It is present in every moment. It is never not always. This Complex has no location because it is everywhere. Being everywhere, it can have no center and all notions of centering or being centered don't make any sense when seen in this light.

Q: That's a bit confusing.

Then let me try to present it differently.

It's like a hole in the paper which is both in the paper and yet not of paper. Likewise, this Complex is at the very center of everything, and yet beyond everything.

Q: That's helpful; I never looked it at like that.

Yes, we have this tendency to look at the small picture and miss out on the big picture. We get completely caught up in this individuality, this reflexive response to everything.

Q; If taking myself for an individual has become a reflex, what can I do about that?

Simply note the mechanism. In seeing it, you are already moving out of it.

The Way One Is

Q: Why am I the way I am?

There are brains-in-bodies with certain qualities and characteristics that are genetic and environmental. So that they can be referred to, they are given a name. In your case, it's Joan.

Joan was given a genetic predisposition, a certain way about herself.

The first time you tasted liver, you had a reaction. Either you liked it or you hated it. A preference was already in place, despite your never having tasted it before. Multiply this by thousands and thousands of hard-wired preferences and you can get a sense of this setup. Increasingly, geneticists are isolating gene sequences that link directly to behavior. Such and such sequence is responsible for such and such behavior.

Personal experience of one's environment modifies these gene sequences. Who one relatively is, so to speak, is DNA plus conditioning. This is Joan's software, her programming.

Q: I can feel myself having a negative reaction to hearing that. (Laughing) That too is part of the programming. Now stay with this. This programming is dynamic in that it is potentially updated by every new experience that comes in. It is the software which responds to the stimulus that is input.

In one moment it will respond to a certain stimulus. Let's say it's your mother calling. You react: "Oh, no, not now". There's a chemical reaction in the brain and a neuromuscular contraction in the body.

An hour later, there have been numerous changes in Joan's biology: blood sugar levels, hormonal balance, etc. All of those things impact her responses. It is not at all impossible that if mom had called that one hour later that Joan's reaction would be entirely different.

This prompts the question, "Who felt aversion?"

Certainly, there was aversion. The aversion appears in the organism because of its programming.

Q: Can I rid myself of any of these behaviors?

Did you put them there?

Q: No

Then it might be best to allow whatever put them there to remove them if and when it sees fit to do so.

Being Roy

Q: Can you tell me what it's like being you?

I'm asked this question often and I always hesitate.

This occurs because I'm concerned if I provide you with a view of what it looks like, that's what you'll go searching for. I don't want that. I want your discovery to be your discovery, not mine.

That having been said, I'll respond this way. There is a subtle sense of joy. I emphasize the word "subtle".

Nothing can toss you from there. Nothing can touch you. It is unassailable.

Whatever appears: thoughts, emotions, dramas of all sorts, nothing pushes you away from it. It can't be improved and it can't be removed. It is constant.

When I interact in the world, there is the experience of the world. That is to say, sometimes it's good, sometimes it's not.

But even this occurs against the subtle backdrop.

Q: Are you saying you never feel sad or angry?

I am decidedly not saintly. There are still moments when I am burdened with a sense of person-hood Therefore, I am subjected to the quirks of it.

Q: What do I have to do to get what you have?

First recognize that you've already "got" it. The things that obscure it only have to be removed.

Q: I don't understand.

All things personal are the obscuration. One truly can't have personal freedom until one is free from the personal. Identification with the "acting body" is the impediment.

Others know this person Roy only by his body, his words and actions. I have knowledge of the person through the body and the sensations, perceptions, thoughts and feelings that arise.

Now if I asked you to tell me what does your mouth taste like, you couldn't answer. There would be no way of knowing unless you eliminated all the foreign or "not-it" tastes that presently reside there. What remained would be what your mouth tasted like.

Similarly, to know what you are, what has to go is what you are not, all those body-mediated sensations, perceptions, thoughts, and feelings. You give up the individuality and you realize the totality.

One Source

Q: If all things in the world appear different, how can I consider all as one?

They may appear to be different, but it doesn't make a difference. In the same tree, we see leaves, flowers, berries and branches, apparently different from one another, yet they are all parts of what comprise 'tree'. Similarly, all things, all organisms are same-sourced and of the same substance.

A gold bracelet and gold earrings may appear to be different, but they are both gold.

They are the same and they are one.

Q: From my perspective, it doesn't seem that way.

Yes, from the personal perspective, it would seem that way.

But I'm asking you to consider a shift in your vantage point. Normally, what is happening is that people assume themselves to be human forms, and they try to understand everything through that filter. They translate whatever I say into the mode of thinking of a personalized human being. People work very hard to protect their dogmas.

That is the trouble.

I'm trying to hold up an alternative mirror, one that reveals you in a new and different view, one that conveys what you truly are.

Q: I don't get it.

Yes, I see that. But not to worry.

It may be that way only for today. Every moment provides another opportunity to see what I'm speaking about.

Being Functional

Perceiving and acting are the functions of the organism. There is no entity, either inside or outside. There is no author, there is no creator of any action or any thought.

Then what is the ego?

Clearly, it is not a fundamental state of being. Is the ego anything more than the drive to be in control, the brain's reaction to experiential overload? Is it any more than the desire for security and therein perpetuity? Is not the personality merely the brain's cumulative adaptation to outside stimuli, a simulation?

The body doesn't care about life and death; in fact, it has no preferences. All concern about life and death is the brain's and its operative extension, me.

If there is no center here, that is that there is no me, then there is no center there, no you, no them, either.

The consequences of this insight are huge. To whom are we directing anger, fear, and jealousy?

Precision Surgery

Q: Surely, I am a person. You can't possibly argue that.

I'll take up the challenge. You're not a person when you're asleep.

Q: Even though I'm asleep, I am.

Yes, you are. But we are talking about being something quite specific, a person. To be a person you must be self-conscious. Is that always the case?

Q: Not when I'm sleeping. Too, I guess, drugged, drunk, delirious or anesthetized

Even when you're awake, are you continually self-conscious?

Q: No, Sometimes I am absent-minded, or just absorbed.

Are you a person during these gaps?

Q: Of course I am. I remember myself as I was yesterday, last month and last year. I'm definitely the same person.

So, to be an unchanging person, you need memory?

Q: Of course.

But without memory, what are you?

Q: Without memory I cannot exist as a person.

Surely you can exist without memory. You do so while sleeping, isn't that so?

Q: I'm alive, but not as a person.

OK, we're making progress. You admit that your existence is only intermittent existence. Now, can you tell me what are you during those intervals when you're not experiencing a person?

Q: Since I am not conscious of myself, I can only say that I exist absent any person.

Can I refer to this existence as impersonal?

Q: All I can say is that I am, but I do not know that I am.

Could you possibly say this about your being unconscious?

Q: No.

You can only describe it in the sense of not remembering some past: "I did not know. I was unconscious."

Q: I was unconscious, how could I remember and what could I remember?

Were you really unconscious, or you just do not remember?

Q: How am I to discern the difference?

Do you remember every second of yesterday?

Q: Of course, not.

Were you then unconscious yesterday?

Q: No

So, you can be conscious and yet you do not remember?

Q: Yes.

Maybe the same applies while you slept, that is to say that you were conscious and just do not remember.

Q: I was asleep. I did not behave like a conscious person.

Again, how do you know?

Q: I was told so by those who saw me asleep.

They could not determine whether you were conscious or not. All they can say is that you were lying quite still with closed eyes and breathing normally.

Q: Yes, I admit that on my own terms I am a person only during my waking hours. What I am in between, I do not know.

This is the first breakthrough, the fact that you know that you do not know.

What the Wind Can Teach

Q: After having listened to you for a while, I think that what you're talking about is all bullshit. Don't talk to me about something Unseen. If I can't see it, I have no interest in it.

That's your prerogative. However, you're missing something important.

Although you can't see the wind, you can come to know it thru its expressions, that is, the movements of the trees, etc.

In the same way, you can come to know this Unseen through Its expressions.

Q: How does any of this benefit me?

The benefit is that it disentangles you from this "me" that has served to limit you.

Without any sense of person-hood, just being, drop all ideas of any I, any me. What can you say about it, without going into your mind to access some definition?

Q: I can't say anything about it.

You can't say anything but you're continuing to function, aren't you? You're still seeing, still hearing?

Q: Yes.

So the functioning is still happening without any mental image. Something is there, an awareness or a sense of presence.

Q: Yes.

What did you have to do to acquire that?

Q: (silence)

You didn't need to acquire it, did you? It is there uncaused, timelessly and ceaselessly, ever always.

Q: I'm still not seeing the benefit.

For the better part of your first two years, there was no sense of "having problems". This is because there was no belief "I am this body". All problems belong to that form only. When the entanglement is severed, all problems dissolve.

See the benefit now?

Soul and Self

Q: I've listened to a number of your talks. Yet, I can't get passed this feeling that there is something inside me, a soul or whatever.

Self-hood emerges when the organism for the first time actively attends to its body as a whole. It is the arising of self consciousness. It wasn't necessary to think nor was it necessary to move. The organism was potentially directed at the world and at itself at the same time. It has become the body as subject.

The feeling of having a body is made up of various subcomponents, the three most important being ownership, agency, and location.

Ownership refers to all things "my". Agency is the author or doer of the actions. So it appears logical that localizing the body would unify the various elements under a single form, so to speak.

At some point in life, this "you" came to exist. Try to recall what it was like for you in the earliest part of your life. When you remember back as far as you can, eventually your memories of yourself end. Your memory of "being" goes no farther back. It just suddenly stops. You may believe that you've always been, yet you have no direct experience of it. You really don't know how it is "you" came to be. Everything becomes conjecture, hearsay, belief. It is not actually a direct personal experience of what's true. You simply don't know; that's a fact.

Yet this is a very important thing not to know.

Q: Without any "me, who makes the choices I must make?

Neuroscience has shown that most processing in the brain is unconscious. We are unaware of routine processes and have little insight into our choices and preferences. Our brains kind of "neurally set up" the decisions we make.

Here's only one example: men prefer photographs of women with dilated pupils. They don't consciously know this but it suggests that male brains rightly or wrongly evolved algorithms to recognize pupil dilation as an indicator of sexual arousal.

The men choosing the most attractive woman, didn't know that the choice was not really theirs. Instead, the choice was made by programs that had been modified and burned into the brain's circuitry over the span of millions of years.

Brains are in the business of gathering information and steering behavior appropriately. Most of what we do and think and feel is not under conscious control. Our brains run mostly on autopilot and the choices that we make are reflective of the software.

Q: I don't believe that.

What you do or don't believe is not what I'm talking about. What do you know, know with certainty?

What we believe, value, and assume, as well as our memory, programming, self-image, and so on, is related to and weighed against our currently perceived circumstance or issue. From this assessment, the internal state that would be most appropriate for relating to those conditions is expressed in a feeling or thought.

I realize that what I am talking about rubs up against what you believe. I am not asking for a single second that you take me at my word.

We have come to believe in forces unseen: gravity, magnetism, electricity, etc. However, most people hesitate to examine this Great Force that I refer to.

Ask yourself: what holds you back from initiating the investigation into the validity or falseness of what I say?

Q: I just don't believe it.

We form our beliefs for a variety of reasons in the context of environments created by family, friends, colleagues, culture, and society at large. After forming our beliefs we then defend, justify, and rationalize them with a host of intellectual reasons, cogent arguments, and rational explanations.

When you say that you don't believe it, that's your fear talking.

Q: Fear of what?

Fear of giving up what you only believe to be true in order to find out what is actually true. Fear of directly confronting the possibility of self deception.

Q: If I were to assume that what you say is accurate, how would I get rid of it?

All fear is personal. To be free from fear, one needs to be free from the personal.

All Conceptual

Make no mistake about it. Everything I say is only a concept. In this case, they are my concepts. They may appear to be my truth but they are not THE TRUTH.

Q: If it's all only conceptual, what's the value in it?

All communication is conceptual. We use concepts to organize our understanding and to communicate.

However, we build concepts upon concepts upon concepts and soon, we become far removed from the actual.

For example, there is seeing. That is the actual. I am seeing is a concept introducing the idea of an agent, "I", into the process. Yet, the concept "I" cannot see. All there is is seeing. However, soon the concept "I" takes on a life of its own. Now, not only does it claim agency, it claims ownership: my idea, my car, my body.

In the end, all "I" is, is an image we have of ourselves, based on past events and experiences and the conditioning that we have received by our parents, society, school, nation and whatever.

From all that, we form this composite which is little more than a pile of concepts.

Concepts are never the actuality. The word "salad" can't be taken in for sustenance.

Movement away from the conceptual and back toward the actual is how we re-establish ourselves as Perception Itself. I'm not saying that concepts have to go. I'm saying that they have to be recognized as something that can only point to the actual, but can never be it. The menu isn't the meal and the map isn't the territory.

Should I Do?

Q: I came to see you because I've been running around quite a bit trying to find an approach to getting clearer about what one might call life's larger questions. But I'm not one inch closer to having a better sense of what I should be doing.

"Should" is a very interesting word, one that is used quite often without an understanding of its underlying supposition. You believe that you "should" be doing something that you're presently not doing. This notion stems from the presumption that you are the source of the doing in the first place, doesn't it?

Q: Why, sure.

Invalidate that presumption and the "should" makes no sense. "Should" can only be applicable to the situation if you have some input to the situation, if you are a source of action, or are responsible for initiating the action.

But, is it so?

Q: I assume it's so.

Let's assume nothing here. What we're looking at is the assumption of being the initiating agent. So, let's direct our attention to see what these assumptions you hold are all about. Let's see if, in fact, you are the source of any doing.

Are you the author, so to speak, or are you an instrument through which whatever gets done merely happens? Is it your act or is it a function of other forces such as your DNA and the effects your environment has had on you? Clearly, if the latter is the case, then your "should" is entirely invalid, isn't it?

Q: I would agree.

I want to make a crucial distinction between being the source of what is happening as opposed to being the instrument through which things happen.

There can be no question that these body/minds with which we're identifying do things. The genetic codes that enable them to do what they do is incredibly complex and powerful.

But where is the evidence that all that is going on is anything more than a complex series of responses to stimuli?

Q: It has to be more than that.

Why?

Q: Because I know that I'm making decisions to do things. That's easy to see.

Todd, you may be surprised to learn that scientific research differs with your findings.

What they have concluded is that about a half second elapses between the time a decision is made and the time when you can say "I decided". That is to say that the decision is made and then, only after the fact, you claim it as your own.

That being the case, the idea of your authorship of the decision is erroneous.

Q: You're saying I don't decide?

I'm saying that I'm the first to admit that it seems that you decide, but, in truth, you don't.

Q: Then who decides?

We could pursue that now but it would take us off track. I want to resolve the issue of your "should".

Wouldn't you agree that if you are not the one that decides, the one that controls what happens, then the idea of what you "should" or "shouldn't" do becomes moot?

Q: It would seem so; yet, somehow it feels incomplete, as if I'm not left with anything.

Well, for one thing, it leaves you without worrying about what you should or shouldn't be doing.

Isn't that enough?

Have a Look

Many of our notions about ourselves and the world are so deeply
implanted into us that we cannot see that they are just beliefs and not
ontological truths.
We believe that:
We have a body
We have a mind
The mind lives somewhere in the body
We are male or female
We are limited
We are in the world
We know how the world works
We were born at a certain time and will die at another time
We are an entity separate from other entities
The entity also lives somewhere in the body
Objects exist independent of their being perceived
We are the subjective aspect of our experience and all else is the
objective
We are the doer of our actions
We are the thinker of our thoughts
We are the feeler of our feelings
We are the choice-maker of our choices
Time and space existed before we were born
The world existed before we were born
Time and space will continue to exist after we are dead
The world will continue to exist after we are dead
Consciousness is something that we have
Consciousness is a personal by-product of the mind and the body
The investigation into these beliefs is a means to discriminating
between what is real and what only seems to be. One simply asks "Is
this true?" It need not be ruthless or constant. It is a gentle looking at
appropriate times and in places. You will find that it will develop a
momentum of its own, independent of how you think it should be.
The way things seem may not change. However, they will no longer
exert such a firm grasp on you as they have been seen through for what
they are.

Stories

Q: What do I need to give up to attain this?

Everything to which "my" applies needs to be defended against loss. Stop defending and see what is lost and what cannot be lost.

Q: And then I will cause this to happen?

You are not the cause of anything. Whether you plan or don't plan, act or don't act, life goes on.

Q: You mean that I should stop demanding a pleasing outcome?

Can you decide to fall in love? Can you decide to beat your heart? These are two processes, out of countless thousands, that go on all the time with neither your involvement nor approval.

The essential question is "Do I control the energy of life or does the energy of life control me? If the answer is the latter, where is the utility of effort?

In the larger sense, it's all a part of the Functioning............... and that's all there really is.

Q: In other words, there are no guarantees.

This I am certain of: once habit patterns, our mechanistic tendencies, are observed, their intensity diminishes. It would not be unusual for them to continue for a while because they have been there for so many years. But the energy that goes into them gets smaller over time and their frequency is reduced. In the absence of energy, like everything else, they die.

This also applies to the Undisputed King of habit patterns: me.

Q: I thought you could give me something more substantial.

Yes, this was your thought. Thoughts come and go. But, I have to be there to receive them before any can arrive. If I pause all the thoughts, do I fall apart? What is still present, with or without thought?

I am present before the mind appears; I am to who the mind appears. I am not the mind. Once the point of view changes, everything changes.

Q: I've been working on myself for a very long time. I came here to improve myself. Now, I feel like I'm coming away empty.

What you were doing before was rearranging the furniture. The time has now come to tear down the walls. There's a vast difference.

You are coming to the end of all becoming. This unsustainable arc of the self improvement story is over, unless you decide to resuscitate it.

Q: Maybe so. But it was a story that had a lot of appeal.

Granted.

However, there is a marked difference between enjoying a fairy tale and believing it.

Total acceptance of what is in every moment is the killer of all fairy tales, of all imaginations. It frees up untold energies; life simply becomes easier.

The bottom line is: right here, right now, I am present and I am aware of being present. All else is an embellishment, an unnecessary fiction. The story it creates is appealing to the brain, but serves little else.

The mind creates scenes within the story. Scene One, Scene Two...... on and on. Thoughts appear, actions occur. Woven together, we create this seemingly coherent narrative.

However, these stories obscure the inherent peace. In the absence of the story, in the absence of thought, one has no problems.

Q: Why then do I still feel so incomplete?

You simply haven't examined it carefully. You are already complete. What needs to be added to completeness?

You are already the final destination.

Spiritual Schizophrenia

Q: As the old expression goes, I'm sick and tired of being sick and tired. My friends told me that they gained some important insights meeting with you, so I came. I'm frustrated with all the unfulfilled promises I've received before.

I'll start out by not making promises of any kind to you. The ocean is here for you. If you bring a thimble to the shoreline, you'll receive very little.

Q: What do you mean by that?

Most people carry all their preconceived notions and ideas about life into this room. They hold their convictions so tightly that their convictions, in fact, hold them. That makes the introduction of a new perspective difficult.

Can you listen without judgment, without immediately drawing conclusions?

Q: I think so.

Good, then let's begin.

When we say "I am cold", "I am bored", "I am tired", "I am thirsty", what is this I referring to? Is it not the body and the mind, the psychosomatic apparatus if you will, and these statements refer to the present state of the apparatus?

Q: I can see that.

When we say "my wife", "my car" etc., the word "my" refers back to mine or that which is of me. What is this me? Is it not the stimulus/response process specific to the "I"? Is it not what we would call the nature of this "I"?

Q: I've never heard it explained that way before, but it makes sense.

How did it acquire this nature? Is it not a combination of the information that was carried on its DNA, in other words, genetics, coupled with the relative quality of its environment, past and present? Is this not then micromanaged via the endocrine system on a moment to moment basis?

When we look at a flower, its form is, so to speak, I. The manner in which it reacts to sunlight, to water, to air pollution, the fragrance it emits, and its pattern of growth are all the "me". Where is the entity? Somehow, we take the I + me and make it into an entity: Ray, the entity. This is the process of reification.

Yet, it is seen that no entity actually exists. What exists is a complex of mechanical processes. When they are taken in sum, they are the person. Yet, no person really exists.

Q: So, once I see this for myself, there's nothing left to do?

There is really nothing to do in the first place. There is no formula you can use to make this happen.

I know of a man who is a well regarded so-called teacher in Europe. His clarity arrived suddenly for him one day while he was taking a walk in the park.

When he shares this story, it is not unusual for him to be asked the name of the park, as people automatically draw the conclusion that his presence in the park had a hand in the whole thing and they want to capture that for themselves.

Q: Now that we're talking about it, I can recall having these briefest of moments where it's all so clear and then I'm back into being me again.

Yes, seeing this and then not seeing this is sort of a spiritual schizophrenia.

Q: And nothing can be done about that either?

You didn't put it there; you can't remove it. Only whatever put it there can remove it.

Q: But I don't know what put it there.

That's OK. But, as such, the entire matter is one less thing for you to worry about. Freeing you of this worry is a movement toward freeing you of all worry.

The Birth of Your Story

It should by now be clear that this "I" is intermittent. I am awake for 16 hours a day. The other 8 hrs are divided between dreaming for roughly two hours and dreamless or deep sleep for six. In deep sleep, there is no I and there is no world. So both are intermittent and are arising in tandem.

Further, this "I" is intermittent in so far as it is not there when fully engaged in working.

What one is is the combination of the genetics, which relates to the body, and memory, which relates to the mind. The mind is the brain's way of protecting itself. When it is perceived that something "outside" may become a threat, fear is born; fear of something from the past projected into the future. This "I" is the brain's response to fear.

Then come the basics: survival, food, clothing and shelter. The movement toward the attainment of these is the beginning of "the story" of oneself.

Into the Unknown

Are we just an experience machine? Do we just continually pump out experiences, one after the other in endless procession?

Helping other people may make you feel good, or seeing a sunset may make you feel vast. Yet, all these are really only biological states. There are specific areas of the brain that are firing. Chemicals are being released.

If you feel alone and disconnected, a different area of the brain lights up; different chemicals are released. As such, experience doesn't happen until the brain creates it.

Q: Are you suggesting that I create a subject, an experiencer, to stand outside of the experience?

Yes I am. It's yet another fabrication taken to be real.

Q: That's pretty cold and impersonal.

You hit the nail right on the head. It's about as impersonal as it can get. But that doesn't make it any less valid.

Q: How does understanding this make any difference?

It may or it may not. It depends on the drive for understanding itself. One of our core neuroses is this need to understand. It is the desire to impose order on that which appears to be disorderly.

The challenge of understanding is that it cannot take place within the known. It can only occur with an exploration of the unknown.

To really do that, you have to leave the safety of the orderly space that you've created for yourself, and jump into the "who-knows-what". You have to stand outside of the understood. This can be terrifying.

Yet, if you are unwilling to make this leap, true understanding cannot occur.

Paying Attention to Attention

For a thing to be known, be it an object or a thought, it must be perceived. For it to be perceived, it must be the focus of attention. This focus is actually the energetic aspect of consciousness. Thus, it is this energy that gives life to thoughts, feelings and perceptions.

When a thing does not receive energy from attention, it ceases to exist. That is why it is said that everything comes and goes. When everything that came has gone, consciousness remains.

Thought that is not sustained by energy is short lived.

Check it out for yourself. A thought that stays with you for more than a few seconds has received the energy of attention. When it no longer has your attention, where is it?

This fixation of attention onto thought takes one away from one's essence. If attention is to be paid, attention should be paid to attention itself.

The Failure of Words

Q: I've noticed that when you speak that there are certain words you don't use, words such as love and God. Why is that?

Communicating verbally is difficult. It is not uncommon for the intended meaning of words to be misconstrued. Let's take the word love for example.

For most people, love is little more than a social contract: I will love you as long as you do what I want and you give me what I want. When that ends, this love turns into something darker, at times, to hate.

So rather than having to repeatedly explain what I would mean by love, I find it more efficient to avoid the use of the word.

The word God carries with it a lot of charge and a lot of meaning. However, the meaning is not homogeneous. Your God and my God are likely to be quite dissimilar. My use of such a word would not facilitate what I am trying to convey.

Possibly the best example of this is the word truth. People talk about speaking the truth. But which truth is it? Is it my truth, your truth, or is it the Truth? Usually, there is an equating of my truth with the Truth. But nothing could be farther from the truth.

(laughter)

You see, every word has at least two meanings. One is the essential meaning, and the other is a personal meaning, that is, it is from a point of view. If you give my word your personal meaning, miscommunication is apt to be the outcome. If one word has got multiple meanings, a whole sentence can be a minefield.

So, for example, when I want to refer to the Source of all things, the Divine, or what have you, rather than use the word God which is so image laden, I use That. When the mind hears That, rather than summon up a palette of images, the mind freezes for a split second.

Q: But using a word like That makes it more difficult for me to understand.

On the contrary, it makes it easier because the word doesn't butt up against the pre-established labels and meanings that the mind has already assigned. To say it in another way, there isn't any cabinet you can immediately file it away in.

Its very freshness is the doorway to the deeper understanding you are seeking.

Q: I've been listening to you for a while now and I've come to the conclusion that what you are saying makes sense.
Thanks, but be wary of reaching conclusions. They may not be indicative of deeper understanding; they may only be a convenient place to stop the investigation.

Promises

Q: What should I expect to get?

I make no promises. I'm not here selling transformation. My purpose is to promote your investigation of the beliefs that you've carried with you for so long and for you to find out if they are, in fact, valid.

Q: And if they are not valid, what then?

Either you'll end up with no beliefs, only certitude, or you'll assign yourself new beliefs.

Q: Let me phrase my question differently. At the end of the investigation, what is present?

There can be many things present, but if I had to select the most important thing present, it would be absence.

Q: What?

It's the absence of all the erroneous beliefs previously held. It's similar to when you take a beautiful rug in to be cleaned. While it's away, you don't see the floor; you only see the absence of the rug. After a while, you begin to see the floor that was always there.

So it's the absence which takes you to what has always been present.

Q: I think my head is spinning a little bit. Could you go over that again?

Maybe it's better to frame it this way: What is your walking like when you no longer have a blister on your foot?

Q: My walking is better.

What do you mean by better?

Q: There is no discomfort.

Might one say that there may still be discomfort, but none if it comes from the blister?

Q: You could, but why are you splitting hairs?

Because I don't want to be misunderstood to be saying that life becomes all perfume and puppy dogs. This is what is generally being sold by the professional gurus and teachers to an unwitting, albeit hungry, audience.

The blister was causing unnecessary ill-ease. The unnecessary goes while whatever is necessary remains.

Q: So there are still problems?

There may or there may not be problems. There is no absolute for the way things will be.

In light of that, how can I make any promises?

Q: When it's all said and done, I may still be miserable.

Maybe you will be. Any guarantees to the contrary would be a deception.

In my experience, if there is a sincere drive, an earnestness, to be free from misery, misery goes. But that earnestness is outside of my control. Therefore, I cannot project a specific outcome.

Q: Well, what the hell. Let's give it a try. All that I have to lose is what I don't want anyway.

We Can't Work It Out

Q: The advice that I should stop thinking frightens me. If I stop thinking, I might as well be dead.

The absence of thought is not dead space. On the contrary, it is vibrancy itself. Absent all labels, all fragments and all concepts, what comes to the fore is what-is. In the absence of thought, what past is there, what future is there? All there is is right here, right now. It is being present to presence.

Don't be afraid to stop thinking, even for just a nanosecond. You won't fall apart. All sensing will continue. The noticing or the registration of everything will continue. In that instant, what is revealed is something vast, something unexplored, yet so vital.

Q: What is it?

The mind content is seen for what it is and what arises is, "I am the seeing, I'm not this content." That's a moment of clarity in which your true essence reveals itself without it being some thing.

Q: Yes, but at some point, the mind kicks back in.

Admittedly, but it doesn't matter what the mind does. You know, whether there is a lot of chatter going on or whether there is complete silence, it doesn't matter because it's neither you nor yours. It's just appearing.

Q: Yet it seems so real, so close to me.

No matter how far you go in the mind it will continue dividing unity into pieces. The first 2 chunks are this seeming you and everything other than you. From there, you just get more and more divisions. When this is understood, it becomes clear that the answer cannot be found in the mind.

It is like sending you to the 7-11 to buy a submarine; you can't get it there.

Without doing anything, the looking there drops away.

Q: I can feel a difference already.

Yes, there was the belief in that Beatles tune "We Can Work It Out". No we can't. No matter how hard we look there, we will never find the answer because the mind doesn't contain it.

Q: It always felt like it was achievable.

Yes it did. Yet, how long are you going to try to work it out until it dawns on you that maybe the answer is not there?

Q: Yeah. It's become obvious that my thoughts aren't holding me together!

Exactly; so if it's not your thoughts holding you together, that means there is something else present that is prior to thought. There's a beingness, something which you can't even grasp or put a label on.

Q: But, how do you go beyond the mind to get to it?

You don't go beyond the mind. There's no place you need to go to. Instead, you realize that right here, right now, you are present and aware, first and foremost. That's before any thought. Poof! You are, so to speak, beyond the mind. Better said, you are before the mind. Where does that leave you?

Q: It leaves me right here, right now, aware of a mind that's trying to grasp onto something.

Yes; so you see that all of the functioning is still happening with or without any mental images to accompany them

Q: That sure removes the hold the images had.

Indeed it does.

When Are You?

Q: It's impossible to stop thinking. It's driving me nuts.
We've established previously that what you are is before the arising of any thought, the awareness of all thought, isn't that so?
Q: Yes
Can you then just stay in the pure Awareness that you are and just watch the thoughts? Can you do that without claiming ownership of the thoughts?
Q: I'll try to but I'm not sure if I can do it.
Of course you can. Can you distinguish between Awareness, which is prior to thought, and thoughts themselves?
Right now, in this moment, aren't you aware when thoughts are appearing, lingering, and dissipating? Even in those nanoseconds between thoughts, in the space of no thought, aren't you still there, aren't you present?
Q: Yes.
OK. So we've established that you remain, with or without thought. This also means that you are not the mind, which is merely the delivery service of thoughts. The mind is not you, it is yours. You can't be what you possess.
Is this clear?
Q: Yes.
Well, this is the real You; there, you have it. It's not going to anywhere nor is it coming from anywhere because it is always present.
Q: It doesn't seem that way.
Understood. But the whole point of this exercise is to clearly discern the difference between the way things seem and the way things are.
Where do you have to go to be where you are? How far do you have to go to be immediately where you are?
Q: Nowhere.
If the mind reveals another thought, it's only another filament in the spider's web. It goes out and then it's drawn back. No reason to give it great power over you. Don't make a big deal out of something that isn't a big deal.
Q: But I don't seem to be able to know that all the time.
Don't worry about knowing it all the time. Know it now; that is enough.

Getting Rid of the Ego

Q: Can you tell me the best way to go forward?

Have you asked others this same question?

Q: Yes, a quite few.

Has anyone told you?

Q: I received answers, but I did not receive any clear or definite answer.

If you did get a clear and definite answer, how would you recognize it?

Q: I don't know. Maybe there is no answer.

Don't back away on this. There is an answer. But if you don't know how to recognize it, what's standing in your way?

Q: I don't know. Maybe one problem is that I can't recognize the obstacles.

If you can't recognize the answer and you can't recognize the obstacles, you've got a bit of a dilemma, don't you?

Q: My ego gets in the way.

Then you can recognize the obstacle.

Q: Yes.

OK, so to restate your original question, you would like to know how to get rid of the ego.

Q: I guess so.

Who is this "you" that wants to get rid of the ego? Isn't it the ego wanting to get rid of the ego?

Q: You make it sound sort of ridiculous.

I wouldn't say it was ridiculous, but as you can see, it isn't a viable strategy.

Q: Then what can I do?

Let us agree that the ego can't rid itself of itself. However, it can learn about where it came from, where it arose from. Would you agree?

Q: Yes, but I'm now feeling lost.

Within your feeling lost is the answer to your dilemma.

To get out from under this feeling of being lost, and to learn more about the origin of this ego, you need to do the same thing: go back the way you came.

Problem Solving

No one comes here because they have too much happiness and it's creating problems for them.

Q: That's funny. Sure, I'm here because of my problems.

That's right. But what is actually going on? That's what we're ultimately questioning.

Any of the assumptions, any of the conclusions that one has brought here, need to be examined. All that examination is a movement towards a deeper, more profound understanding that is not contingent on anything else.

Q: But these problems must serve some purpose. Are they there to spur my growth? I guess I'm really asking why are they here?

The answer to any "Why" question will do nothing to move you closer to peace and understanding. "Why" is mind only. "Why" is a story, food for the mind.

Q: You're supposed to be the expert. I am here so you could help me solve my problems.

I'm not expert in problem solving. My area of expertise, if one truly exists, is in not-knowing.

Q: What do you mean?

For as long as you don't know that you don't know, nothing can change. The first step is knowing that you don't know and that can't occur until you examine what it is that you believe you know.

Q: I'm 43 years old. There's a lot that I know.

It's not my place to argue the point with you.

Suffice it to say that all this supposed knowledge hasn't helped you solve these problems of yours. If you don't want to examine the validity of all this knowledge, then let's at least for the time being set the knowledge aside and try to find another mode or approach that can be helpful to you.

Is that fair?

Q: Sure.

OK; so what are the problems that you want help with?

Q: Do you want the whole list?

That would depend on how lengthy it is. Let's start with four.

Q: Fine

I'm not happy about getting older. I'm worried about finances. I'm dissatisfied with my job. I'm getting divorced. Will that do?
Of course.
Let's begin, then, by identifying what is common to all four. Can you tell me what that is?
Q: No
What is common to all four is I. In the absence of this I, the problems dissolve.
Q: This is just semantics. This I can't be absent.
All words can be faulted; only silence is faultless. But that can't help you until you are ready to hear it.
This I is, in fact, absent often throughout the day and night. It is absent when there is deep involvement in a task. It is absent while dreaming and in dreamless sleep. It comes and goes like any other phenomenon. The only difference is that this I is totally without substance of any kind.
A phenomenon without substance is typically referred to as a ghost; that's applicable here.
Q: You're saying I am a ghost?
No, I is a ghost. What you are is something else entirely.

Getting There

We're not talking about working on the person, on some sort of self-improvement.

Instead, what is addressed here is seeing through the personal.

Q: I have been doing that for more than a decade. I still haven't arrived there.

It is the very idea of "there" that holds you back. It is the construction of a journey, going from some predefined "here" to an idealized "there". It's more mind stuff.

Here's your hypothesis: You can't see yourself from here. Maybe if you walk over there, you can see yourself from there. Can you see the zaniness of it?

Setting another trap can never get you out of a trap.

Q: But I feel that I've made progress.

In getting to where?

Q: To seeing through the personal.

I think we need to be careful here because there is a tendency to misunderstand.

Linda, did you ever feel that you were making progress toward seeing that you were a woman?

Q: No, I just knew it.

Seeing through the personal works in much the same way. It doesn't occur in bits and pieces. Either you see it or you've yet to see it. When you see it, there is conviction behind it. It resides in your core and requires no proof or validation of any kind.

Q: I see, so I haven't gotten it yet. God knows, I may never get it.

(laughing) Let's stay with your reference to God; God sends thoughts to you. You believe you are thinking. God moves you to act; you believe the actions are yours.

Seeing through your assumptions to the reality lying beneath them is what we're talking about…… and you can do that here and now. No "there" to get to, only here.

Q: I've read so much, done what seems to be like endless practices. It's all resulted in a big, fat zero. I'm feeling so disillusioned.

You've chosen to use an interesting word: disillusioned. Actually, if you were disillusioned, all this running around would be over. Disillusioned is the breaking of illusion, is it not?

The illusion is believing that the appearance is the way things are. Disillusionment is the seeing the way things are.

Q: You twist all my words around on me. Maybe it would be better if I just kept quiet.

Yes, keeping quiet is an excellent posture. From it, what needs to arise to reveal itself can do so without having to contend with all the mental noise.

Good choice!

Nothing New Here

There's nothing new here. What I'm talking about is the same thing that the mystics have been claiming for thousands of years.

So, if you've already rejected the message of the mystics, you'll probably be disappointed here.

Q: Just so I'm clear on what you're referring to, what is their message?

The message that has been handed down throughout the ages by the mystics, by the sages and by the saints of all religions is you are not what you seem to be. You are That on which everything appears and disappears.

Ask yourself this: Upon awakening in the morning, what wakes up first?

Q: I have no idea what you're talking about.

Don't you find that the sense being, of aliveness, of I-am, appears first? Then I-am-such-and-such; lastly, the world appears. It all happens in the space of a finger snap. Check it out for yourself. Don't take my word for it.

Q: OK, I see what you're trying to say. Please continue.

This simple observation prompts some very intriguing questions:

To whom, or maybe better stated as "to what", do these appear?

What is it by which one knows that one is?

What can be said about the world once it is acknowledged that the one who knows the world precedes it?

Q: That's some deep stuff.

It needn't be; yet, it is admittedly very powerful. In many, it has spurred the desire to look more deeply into some very closely held assumptions about oneself.

Q: Can you give me an example?

Sure. Sometime around the age of 2, the brain has developed sufficiently so that it can begin to organize experience. Self-consciousness or "me" becomes that organizing point of reference. The mind fragments wholeness, first into subject and object, then further into infinite objects. It is a process, functioning as translation or cognition, memory or re-cognition and reaction. Body, too, is a process, functioning as sensing and acting.

When this is fully understood, the obvious conclusion is that there is no entity at work. What is taken for an entity is merely this mechanism, this complex of processes working through a form. What we refer to as personality is a description of this complex.

At best, Jeremy is then only an address, a place we can look at in order to see the processes that he is the manifestation of.

Q: That's what you've reduced me to, a process? What about my thoughts, my feelings?

They're all part of the process whose end result is Jeremy doing what Jeremy does.

If you give me a bit of linguistic leeway, let's concede that feelings are thoughts, OK?

Q: Sure.

We know that you don't create the thoughts, that you don't have a say in their content. You simply receive them. Where they come from we can address at another time.

The thoughts come and they tweak the process that is Jeremy. Thoughts yield to other thoughts and some thoughts spur action.

Where is this entity "you" in all this?

Q: I don't know. But I intend to look for it some more rather than just assume you know what you're talking about.

I wouldn't have it any other way.

Many Questions, One Question

What am I, really?

Am I my body?

Am I my thoughts and feelings?

Am I all the sensations that I perceive?

Am I my identity, the total of everything that I identify with?

Am I the awareness of my identity?

Am I my personality, the way I act and react?

Am I the image I have of myself?

Am I this narrator, endlessly speaking to me inside my head?

Am I this film of memory that gives me a sense of continuity, of being always present?

Am I the amalgam of my socio-cultural conditioning and genetic programming?

Am I an independent, autonomous center of volition?

Am I the imagined main character in this play called Life?

Am I all of these?

Am I none of these?

Am I something else not yet acknowledged?

What am I, really?

No Thingness

Q: I'm looking for a way to put an end to all my dissatisfaction. I've been rushing around for years trying to find a way to do it.

Meister Eckhart, a 12th-13th century German Christian mystic, said: "For whoever seeks God in some special way, will gain the way and lose God who is hidden in the way. But whoever seeks God without any special way, finds Him as He really is."

I am not saying that you are seeking God, and I don't want to get hung up with that whole concept. But you are rushing after something.

I maintain that there is no special way needed to find it. Just have a look, that's all.

The discovery of what you really are, your true being, is the so-called destination. You only rush to a destination until the time when you reach it. Then the rushing ceases.

Since this true being is here and now, I am glad to tell you that you've already arrived at your destination.

So, stop all your rushing and relax.

Q: Your pronouncement doesn't change anything. I feel the same as I felt before.

I wouldn't expect it to be otherwise. For as long as you identify with feelings, with thoughts…….. if this is what you believe yourself to be………… this bundle, then yes, nothing changes.

But when you step outside of it, when you realize that what you are is the screen onto which all this appears, then the feelings, good or bad, lose that charge that held you so tightly.

Q: Do I stop feeling?

Oh, no, the feelings continue. What is different is that you can observe them without taking them to be yours.

Q: If they are not mine, whose feelings are they?

The process whereby we take something and make an entity out of it when it requires no entity is called reification. That's what you're doing here. The question of "Who?" need not come up.

The feeling of anger arises; that's it. There is anger. Finished!

Q: No "who"?

No "who".

Q: The anger then just goes away?

Let's say that it doesn't linger as long since there is no one holding on to it and claiming it as their own.

Q: If I were to do that with every feeling and thought that came up, I'd be reduced to nothing.

Yes, and that is exactly where I am trying to take you. I am trying to take you to that place where you are no thing in particular.

Q: I don't think I understand.

Let's try a few images. These images are, of course, of things. But I think they'll help you to see my point, OK?

Q: OK

I'm saying that you are the sky. Clouds come, clouds go. The sky doesn't complain that it is cloudy; it remains unaffected.

I'm saying that you are the ocean. Waves arise, waves crest and disappear. The ocean doesn't complain about the swells; it remains unaffected.

Q: That sounds all well and good. But that's not how I see things.

Of course not, because if you saw things from that perspective, you wouldn't be dissatisfied and you wouldn't be here.

What I'm trying to bring about is a metanoesis, a change in viewpoint. Nothing more.

Inside Your Head

Q: I know I'm not the body. I am whatever it is that watches the body change over the course of time, while I have remained unchanged. Yet I see things only from this point of being inside the body.

Yes, primarily there is that registering of everything. Just like that mirror on the wall is reflecting everything in front of it, so there is "something" registering everything. You heard that siren before you labeled it a siren. You are hearing this voice, seeing the sights in the room, feeling your body standing against the wall.

All the thoughts are being registered also. Do you feel like you are in any specific location inside the body where all this is going on?

Q: Let me think about that.

Do you feel that you are located above your waist or below your waist?

Q: Oh, definitely above it.

Do you feel you are above the neck or below the neck?

Q: I'm above the neck, in the head.

Where?

Q: Behind the eyes.

Do you have a shape? How large are you?

Q: About a half an inch wide, kind of round.

Is it on the left, right, or in the center behind the eyes?

Q: I feel like I'm in the center behind the eyes.

How far back?

Q: Not sure..........not much.

So you're a pea-sized ball about a half inch behind the center of your eyes!

Q: Yeah, sure (smirking)....

To what does this pea appear?

Q: What?

Does the pea appear as an image?

Q: Yes it does!

So if this image is appearing, what perceives it?

Q: I've got it; this pea isn't the seer - it is being seen. I guess it's just an idea I have of myself.

Yes, the fact that all the sense organs are located in the head makes us think that this is where we are. Now, let's return to the pea image, and the awareness of the pea image. Do you feel as if you're seeing it or do you feel as if you are being seen?

Q: I feel that I'm looking at it. I'm outside.

As the seeing arises, does it have a specific location?

Q: I can only say it must be in the brain, but that's just my idea of it. The experience itself doesn't have any location at all.

So what we have is a non-local locus of awareness that is always present.

It can be said to be nowhere yet everywhere. If it is everywhere, then there is no place it is not. Therefore, it can't be exclusively outside you, nor can it be exclusively inside you. It is better to understand it as that presence-awareness which permeates everything and, as we have seen, you are That.

No Shepherd, No Sheep

In essence, what I am trying to set forth is the state of affairs. But, don't take my word for it. Don't be a sheep to be herded around. I have no interest in being a shepherd.

Look for yourself.

Q: This is not a subject that is easily understood, but I'm trying.

An understanding is most likely from the position of the single activity that remains when the apparent separation between subject and object has been dissolved. I recognize that understanding without this dualistic relationship may be a foreign idea. Perhaps it can be glimpsed if we compare it to the relationship between a thought and the thinker of the thought.

Such a division is only a grammatical convention. There is never a thought independent and exclusive of a thinker. Thought and thinker make up a single process called thinking. Likewise, the one who understands and that which is understood can be seen as the two poles of understanding. Once the "understander" and the understood merge, no one is left to "get it". There is only understanding.

Q: Why am I having so much trouble with this?

We are shifting the locus of attention from the personal to the impersonal, to the totality. What you are trying to do is to examine the totality from outside of the totality. You can't do that; how can you stand outside of everything?

Q: Then this investigation is set up to fail.

Yes, it must fail as long as you get to set the parameters of how the investigation proceeds.

Q: How am I doing that?

You are insisting in framing everything within the context of entities, of a thinker, an understander, a you. Instead, look from the standpoint of processes: thinking, understanding, reacting, etc.

I believe that you will find this viewpoint to be not only different, but quite revealing. Continue to do this and you will find that you can ease into it readily and your much sought after understanding will deepen.

Q: Do you have any tips for me?

Let's start from an undeniable baseline: you are conscious.

What exactly is this consciousness? Let's not try to define it just yet other than to be clear that, for the moment, it is entirely distinct from everything you are conscious of.

Can we agree that you never can say, "There is no Consciousness" because you must already be conscious in order to say it?

Q: Of course I'm conscious. That's an obvious fact.

But what does that mean? In the absence of this consciousness, you wouldn't be able to say there is such a thing as this room, or the people inside it.

In the absence of this consciousness, nothing could be said to exist, not even Life itself. In fact, one couldn't even be conscious of any sort of nothingness. Therefore, your consciousness of your world is all there is to your world.

Now direct your investigation to that place that separates this consciousness and yourself. Where is it located? What are its properties? Does it begin and end?

That should get you on your way.

Thinking About Thoughts

Q: Are we going to be analyzing my thoughts?

No we're not. But let's first take a step back.

At some point between 18-24 months in the infancy of a child, self consciousness arises. This is the sense of a "me" that is separate and distinct from the environment it finds itself in. It is expressed by the thought "I am". This thought is then the foundation for all of the other thoughts that follow: I am happy, I am sad, I am not good enough, I am too fat ....and on and on.

However, the key point that is overlooked is that thought is not born in the brain any more than a radio creates sound. It is merely transmitted through it.

My concept is that we're receptacles picking up signals from elsewhere; there is nothing in our current scientific knowledge that rules this out. Thus, the brain is not an originator, but instead, a receiver/transformer.

Q: You can say it any way that you want, but whatever comes up are clearly my thoughts.

What is it about them that makes them yours?

Q: They come into my head; I hear them.

You hear the beautiful song of a bird; that doesn't make it your song, does it?

Q: OK, I mis-spoke. I don't hear them. I'm aware of them.

Fine, but you're making the leap from being aware of something to claiming it as your own. You are aware of so many things, yet you don't claim ownership of them. What makes the thoughts that come "yours"?

Q: I thought them.

We've already seen that's not the case. You merely received them.......
And the truth is that you have no control over what comes. Can you tell me what your next thought is going to be?

Q: No, I can't. But I know that they're important.

Are they? Those things that are important to us we usually remember, don't we? How much time will you need to tell me what thoughts came to you yesterday? Can you even fill up a single minute with your reply?

Q: Wow, you're really blowing my mind. So what am I supposed to do with all these thoughts that come?

Treat them like letters that have been delivered to you in error. When they don't receive the energy of attention that they previously enjoyed, their hold on you dissipates.

Q: Are you saying that there is nothing positive about thinking?

There is thinking and there is functioning, distinct from thinking. There is reacting and there is responding, outside of the process of thought.

Functioning or process occurs through the workings of an intelligence-energy dyad, consciousness and the life-force. I often call it The Complex.

It is effortless and natural. Cells are replaced, wastes are eliminated, what needs to be done gets done. The entirety is self-regulating. Whether one calls it God, Brahma, Buddha-nature, Yahweh, prana, qi, etc. is of no importance.

When action is required, it can be facilitated via thought. Matters such as planning can be a thought process. However, most thinking reflects the programming for survival, for continuity, which manifests through the psychosomatic unit and is me-based.

Q: Therefore, you're saying that thoughts are the problem and thinking needs to be stopped?

No, I'm not.

First, who is to stop the thinking? We've already agreed that you don't control it.

Thoughts come and go. Through it all, you remain present and know all of them. The thoughts can be endless; following them is a movement away from this presence.

What I'm saying is that the streaming of thought is not the problem; taking ownership of the thoughts is the problem.

Q: After I left you last time, thoughts did not seem to have the charge they usually have.

That is because what I am pointing to and what you are resonating with is this naturalness which is inherently free of thought. It is not hard to recognize at all, once attention is turned away from the content that is appearing.

What Changes?

Q: You talk about this clarity as if it is accessible for all of us. I find that hard to believe.

Clarity is not the exclusive territory of the gurus or the so-called enlightened beings. Nobody is excluded from it. It's as simple as that. Exclusion presupposes that some sort of boundary has been established, a boundary that allows those special ones in and keeps everyone else out. But once Oneness is recognized, the idea of a boundary to Oneness becomes laughable. Oneness is the negation of all boundaries.

Q: Can it really be as simple as that?

Most definitely. Within this, your spiritual experiences or your religious hierarchies lose their preferred status. Worship isn't higher up than driving a bus.

There is no quality of holiness about it; it is completely neutral. Recognition of it will not turn you into someone special because it cannot be related to goodness or specialness. It is beyond all that.

It becomes apparent that the separate you is a ghost. Then, the seriousness about the personal story drops away. You no longer see yourself as spiritual; that stuff especially loses all its zing. There is a lightness to life, without any predefined characteristics of how it should be.

Q: What, then, is different?

All the images of the personal story still continue to appear, but they are seen for what they are. But they are not what we are. This is the clarity.

The whole appearance of what we call our person acting in the world will apparently go on and on, the rules of society will still be there, but it is now seen as one majestic movie.

In that movie, the voice-overs that you experience as an inner voice, what some call mind and I call brain-speak, may also continue.............. or they may not.

Q: Should I meditate? Many teachers prescribe meditation; they say that it is effective for attaining this clarity.

Effective to whom, to that phantom?

Q: Some people claim to have reached this understanding after concerted meditation.

What about all these people who meditated for decades and still say they haven't gotten "it"? Their teachers tell them that they haven't gotten "it" because of some defect in themselves or their practice. But that stance is merely self-serving.

Many others actually say the opposite. They believe they got "it" because they grew tired of the lack of results. They argue that "it" happened when they gave up meditating. Looking back, they suggest that the purpose of meditation is to see its futility.

Q: I can see your point. Some of my friends have literally spent decades at the feet of a guru, and indeed, they're still searching for "it".

You can go to some of the most so-called spiritual locales in the world. Maybe you'll have transcendental experiences or maybe you'll just have severe diarrhea. But chasing after experiences is not the answer.

There is nowhere that you have to go to see this.

Stop the chasing, stop the running after something that you believe will give "it" to you. Instead of reaching out after anything which you deem absent, discover that which is already here.

Look at what is present and available, right here, right now. That is all that is required.

Deconstruction

What we want to do here is to reduce the number of beliefs that we hold to as close to zero as we can.

Q: Why would you want to do that?

What is a belief? A belief is something that we hold as a fact without the concrete evidence to support it. We want to expose how many of our beliefs are actually facts as opposed to personal points of view.

If we know the sun rises in the east, we can willingly entertain challenges to this belief, because it is a fact. But if we merely believe the sun rises in the west, then the challenge to our belief is also a challenge to our belief structure. Usually, we react to this with dismissal or avoidance saying "I have faith that the sun rises in the west."

I would reply "Why not see for yourself?"

Q: But I know that what I believe is true.

How can it be true if it's never been verified?

That's the safety in believing; it requires no authentication. It can be defended, it can be strengthened through conditioning, it can be expanded through coercion, but belief will never stand up and demand proof. Belief can never take the risk that falsity will be revealed.

Many of our ideas and beliefs about ourselves and the world are so deeply ingrained that we are unaware that they are beliefs and take them, without questioning, for the absolute certainties. As such, one's reality is determined by one's beliefs.

Q: If I understand you, the end result will be that there will be new and better knowledge of everything; is that right?

The investigation into the nature of ourselves and of the world of objects initially has more to do with the exposure of deeply held ideas and beliefs about the way we think things are, than of acquiring any new knowledge. It is the exposure of our false certainties.

Q: We'll be rejecting certain beliefs?

Those beliefs that we can substantiate become facts. Those that we mistakenly held to be a fact, once exposed, drop away naturally.

What we're then left with is what really is, not what we have imagined or believed.

Q: I'm intrigued. Where do we begin?

We begin by deconstructing the one believed to be the believer.

Q; When you speak about deconstructing "the believer", I'm a bit fuzzy on what you mean. Could you explain?

The notion of a separate entity, referred to in language as "me", "my" or "I", is quite common. Yet we rarely take the time to ask for clarification on what these terms really refer to. We assume that it refers to, for lack of a better description, this body/mind. In the spirit of bringing no preconceived assumptions into our investigation, it is important that we take a look.

So let's begin with the body.

We readily say "my body" and assume that it is part of me. But is it? When we say "my car", does that make your car a part of you? When we say "my dog", does that make your dog a part of you? Of course not. Therefore, using the "my" qualifier, of and by itself, does not help to define what you are.

When this is seen, all the "my's" become disqualified: my thoughts, my feelings, my self image, my opinions, my life story, etc.

Q: My God, there's nothing left!

That's almost true; the cupboard is admittedly pretty bare. Now, let's reorganize things just a little so that we can better move forward.

Let's break down the totally of your life into three baskets. In the first, there is the experience of all objects that, when taken as a whole, constitute the world. In the second, we place all sensations that arise and, when taken as a whole, constitute the body. In the last, we place all thoughts that come and, when taken as a whole, constitute the mind. Are you with me?

Q: Yes, three baskets: the world, the body, and the mind.

We can talk about my mind, my body and even my world. But as we have seen, any "my" is not what you are. What belongs to you is not what you are.

What you are is the screen, so to speak, onto which these all appear, possibly linger, and then dissolve.

This screen is completely unaffected by what appears on it. In a cinema, they may be playing a movie featuring a tsunami. Yet, the screen remains dry............... or in the case of an inferno, the screen is not charred. In that sense, the screen remains neutral, unaffected by whatever appears on it.

Q: What do you call this screen?

This screen is only a metaphor, so naming it would be a movement away from what it points to, a placing into some conceptual box. "Screen" is enough of a concept on its own. I'd rather focus on its attributes or qualities.

Without making assumptions of any kind, what we know about ourselves with absolute certainty is that we are present and aware. This cannot be challenged. Even to say "I am not" fails to negate it.

We can also say that there is an intelligence there. Therefore, this that we are referring to as a screen has the attributes of an intelligent awareness that is always present.

Lastly, it is what registers everything that appears before it. Not only is it the known, it is also that which knows. It is the resolution of the subject/object, the knower and the known, into the Oneness of Knowing or Pure Subjectivity.

This is the sum of what needs to be seen. It is overlooked because it is so subtle, yet so obvious.

Q: I'm still not putting the pieces together. There is this screen that you refer to and then there is this person, Jill. What is the connection between the two?

I'm not sure that "connection" is the proper word to use. Jill is what appears on the screen. Jill is the object appearing to its subject wherein the screen is the pure subjectivity. Right now, you place all of your attention on the object, Jill, and ignore the subject. In so doing, there is identification with the object.

Q: If a shift were to occur in me, how would my experience of life be any different?

Jill's problems would no longer be yours.

The Strategy of Subtraction

There is a feeling of incompleteness, a feeling of deficiency. Something seems to be missing. When this arises, the so-called Search begins. Since the sense of lack is felt on the inside, we initiate the searching on the outside. As we feel that we are not enough, we want to add more, acquire more, gain more. This is the Strategy of Adding. Yet, whatever the more may be, more money, more prestige, more love……. it does not satisfy.

Possibly, the search takes a different path. Instead of adding more, we seek to enhance what is there. This is the Strategy of Improvement and it takes the form of psychotherapy or the modalities of the Human Potential movement. However, here again, regardless of whatever relative successes are made, something still feels missing, incomplete. That is because the understanding of what can supply the remedy is absent.

The root of the problem lies in what has already been added, what has already been acquired. Therefore, the strategy of continuing to add is bound to fail. The strategy of improving on it is likewise bound to fail. Let's then try a new strategy: the Strategy of Subtraction.

The central hypothesis behind this strategy is that what has already been added masks or obscures our essence, what we truly are. This essence is whole and complete and, as such, has no deficiencies. Seeking it out, so to speak, obliges us to distinguish between the essence and the add-ons.

Q: I'm not clear on what you mean when you speak about add-ons. What has been added on?

Everything that you refer to as mine, for which you use the word my, constitutes the add-ons.

Let's take a single example: my body. This body is an object that you are aware of. In that sense, it is no different than a chair and cannot be what you are.

Q: Whoa! Slow down. I disagree. This is my body; it is part of what I am.

What makes you say this with such certainty?

Q: Because I've known it all my life.

You know, that statement isn't entirely accurate. It wasn't until self-consciousness arose in you that you began to assume that the body was part of what you are. This was then reinforced by your parents, your teachers and your society.

I'm not suggesting that you reject your belief out of hand. I'm only asking that you check it out for yourself. It is the unexamined that keeps us in our prisons. It is the same unexamined that, once examined, can set us free.

Q: OK, I'll hang in there with you.

Good. For the one moment that you are willing to assume that you are not this body, how does your relationship to it change?

Q: Something does seem to shift, but I can't put my finger on it.

Could I say that the energetic hold that it had on you has shifted, has diminished?

Q: As a matter of fact, that's how it feels.

Therefore, you are less preoccupied with it.

Q: Yes.

Now imagine, if you would, that the same shifting occurred for all the my's that you lay claim to. How freeing would that be? Don't you feel less constricted in simply giving it consideration?

Q: Wow! That's amazing.

That's really the Strategy of Subtraction in a nutshell. As the various mine's are removed, your essential nature is more and more revealed. This nature is the fullness and completion that all the searches have been about.

In the end, all this time you have only been searching for your Self.

What's Not Yours

Jesus wasn't a Christian; he was a Jewish rabbi. Buddha wasn't a Buddhist; he was a Hindu prince.

These are merely labels and all that labels do is to divide and make us lose sight of what we essentially are. They literally and figuratively blind us.

Q: Why do we do that? Why do we label everything?

When something is perceived for the first time, it is not labeled. It is merely cognized. There is no for-or-against in it. When the second perception of it occurs, it is re-cognized and that is when the label is applied so that it may be accessed for future reference. We call it recognition.

The labels may have multiple layers such as bad feeling/loneliness or sunset/beautiful.

Q: I can see that. I can remember times of feeling lonely and saying to myself "I don't want this".

In that, there is the invitation to check out who is talking to whom.

Q: I'm not following you.

What I want to do is to look at the statement before labels were assigned, before preconceived notions or beliefs were attached to it.

Q: OK

At its most basic, the statement "I don't want this" suddenly appears from an unknown source and is perceived by something subjective. This much is undeniable, wouldn't you agree?

Q: What do you mean unknown source? I thought it.

Did you really? Tell me, where do you create thought?

Q: In my brain.

The brain has no means to create thought. It receives thought, it transmits thought, but there is no evidence that it creates it.

Q: Where does that leave us?

We return back to my original statement, and my asking you about its undeniability.

Q: Yes, it's undeniable.

We know that this subjectivity cannot have a form because if it did, it would be an object and could not be the subjectivity, right?

Q; Why can't there be a subjective object?

There can't be a subjective object for the same reason that the tongue can't taste itself. There is the tongue, which is the objective, and there is the tasting, which is the subjective, the knowing, the perceiving. The object ultimately cannot know the subject.

Q: Gotcha.

Good; now where does the thought "I don't want this" appear?

Q; It appears in my mind.

Where is that located?

Q: Inside my head.

Are you certain of that or might it only seem that way because most of your senses are located there? If all your senses were located in your right knee, might it seem that the mind was located in your knee?

Q: Well I guess it could. Now that you ask, I don't really know where it's located.

Fine, let's continue on. The thought "I don't want this" has arisen and has been perceived. Now, who is this "I" that it refers to?

Q; Me

This would be the "me" that made the thought "mine", I would presume?

Q: Yes

What is that?

Q: Me? (pause) That's my body, my mind, my intellect, my habits. I'm sure there's more but I feel like I'm in the hot seat.

Surely you can see that anything that belongs to you can't be you, can't be what you are? In that sense, "my body, my mind, my intellect, my habits" are no more you than "my motorcycle, my boss, or my opinions".

Let's sum it up: a thought appeared from an undefined location, appeared to an undefined subjectivity and referenced a John through the use of the word "I". This we can agree on.

Yet, it must be obvious that this John, this "my body, my mind, my intellect, my habits" is another object. Therefore it can't be the subjective, the perceiving of the appearance. It can't appear to John.

Q; I know that this must be going somewhere but I can't see it.

The thought appears and it is perceived. What you are is the perceiving subjectivity, not John the psychosomatic unit or object. You are the aware screen, so to speak, on which everything appears. The fixation on the stories that are shown on John TV, the dramas, the comedies, the tragedies, etc., is where all the difficulty comes from.

Q: Are you saying it isn't real?

There are stories playing; the plots are admittedly engaging. In fact, it's quite a presentation. All I'm saying is continue to watch the stories if you want to; just don't make them yours.

When they are no longer yours, the emotional charge that they carried before isn't there anymore.

Q: Where does that leave John?

He remains as he was before, the play's protagonist.

Experiencing Yourself

Paul, I want to thank you for volunteering for this little experiment. What I would like for you to do is to look out of this window at the apple tree. Continue to look at it for about 30 seconds and then tell me your experience of it. OK?

Paul: OK.

(30 seconds later) Now, what is your experience of it?

Paul: It is tall and green. It has many branches and leaves. On some of the branches, apples are growing.

Is there anything else?

Paul: No, I guess that's about it.

OK. Now, let's shift our attention to something else. For the next 30 seconds, Paul, I want you to sit quietly and experience yourself. Then, tell me your experience.

(30 seconds later) What can you say Paul?

Paul: My hair is turning gray and I am putting on a few pounds. My body feels a little tense sitting still in the chair.

Good. Is there more?

Paul: I am a little nervous. My heart is racing a bit. I have some concerns about a speech I must make later in the week.

Fine. Are there more general things you can tell me about Paul?

Paul: He is concerned about others, sometimes to a fault. He is very analytical, thinks too much and worries about the future.

Anything else? Is this your picture of this so-called you?

Paul: Yes, for now, that's it.

OK, thank you for being brave enough to do this.

Let's notice that if we extend the experience of you for periods longer than 30 seconds, it seems to be fairly continuous. What we do then is we take it and make a narrative out of it, your story, the story of Paul so to speak. Is that clear?

Paul: Yes it is.

So when we speak about Paul, we are only referencing this narrative. This is a key point. You is an experience.

For the time being, let us not add any embellishments onto the narrative. Let us not automatically assume that there is an entity there. Let us simply continue on with this line of investigation.

Now this story had an experience of an apple tree. Can you agree that this makes no sense once we acknowledge that the story is just another experience? How can an experience have an experience?

Paul: Well, yes, I guess it so.

Clearly, there were experiences. What is less clear is what was having them.

Can we find a boundary that divides the experience from that which is having the experience?

Paul: Yes, I can. My body.

Was it your body that was having the experience of your body in the chair or was it something else?

Paul: I can't say. Maybe it was my mind.

Stop for a moment. Isn't your mind just another experience? Isn't your body just another experience? What experiences them?

(silence)

What I am trying to do is to spur the investigation into the nature of experience and into what or who has the experience.

If we can't find a boundary between the experience and the so-called experiencer, maybe there isn't one. What if the experience and the experience are one indivisible whole, a unified field of aware-energy? Is this unified field itself not the support of every experience in the same way that the paper is the support of every printed or written word? Does anything new need to be added to a page in order to see the paper? Does anything new need to be added to this current experience in order to become aware of the unified field that is its support?

Do the words themselves affect the paper? Does it matter to the paper what is said in the words? Does water care whether or not it quenches your thirst? Does the content of each experience in any way affect the unified field in which it appears?

When we return to the words, having noticed the paper, do we lose sight of the paper? Do we not now see the apparent two simultaneously as one? Did we not always already experience them as one, without realizing it?

Paul: If what you say is the case, that means that I, that is Paul, am the writing on the paper. In accepting that, I can feel a seriousness about myself falling away.

Now you're getting it.

Scaling the Great Wall

Sometime around the age of 2 or so, we become self-conscious and, in so doing, we erect our first wall, so to speak.

It is the wall that separates the sense of a separate self, a me, from everything else. It is the line of demarcation between the organism and its ecology. From there, we make the seemingly simple leap of defining the entirety of experience as either inside or outside; it is me in here and objects out there.

Of all the walls we construct, the one between me and not- me is the most fundamental. We have invested years to fortify it, to repair it when necessary, and to defend it. It is the wall we are most reluctant to surrender. It is the first one we draw and the last one we are willing to relinquish at the time of death.

Further, it is the wall that is the foundation for all of the other walls we erect. We must first distinguish ourselves from things before we can distinguish between things.

Q: Granted that these walls exist. But aren't they a good thing? Don't they serve to protect us?

On an elementary level, what you say is correct. However, on a deeper level, all walls are obstacles to unity. Locking things out also locks you in. In unity, there is nothing one needs protection from.

Q: Wow! Tearing all those walls down one by one is a life's worth of work.

If we had to tackle all of our walls separately, one by one, that would be right. But since all of our other walls depend upon this primary wall for support, if we take it down, we take them all down. The entire structure collapses; that greatly simplifies our work.

Once the structure collapses; the space remains. It is this space that I am.

The truth is that we don't even really need to tear it down. What we need to do is become so completely aware of it that it becomes transparent. Then, it is seen through. As such, whether or not it continues to arise is of less importance.

It no longer rules you.

Q: How do I do that?

Yes, it always comes down to the how-to.

I say treat it as you would treat any other habit that you are trying to break, because the truth of the matter is that believing that there is a person inside of this body is only a habit. Admittedly, it is deeply ingrained; but it is a habit nonetheless.

Q: Are you reducing my personality to mere habit? I'm not comfortable with that.

If the goal is maintaining your comfort level, then any sincere investigation should be abandoned.

However, if you are willing, take a minute and look into the notion of personality. What is it? Is it not a process by which information is received and reacted to? Is it not fairly repetitive to the point of habitual?

Q: I guess it is. But if the person is only a habit, who is to see that it's only a habit?

That's the paradox. Dividing seeing into seer, seeing and seen creates it. It's more wall building. There is seeing only.

(laughing) Seeing this is the first step in seeing the habitual.

The Source of Unhappiness

Q: I've been so unhappy for quite a while now. Nothing seems to be getting better. Can you put an end to this?

I see this often. Wanting happiness is the very evidence of unhappiness. I cannot put an end to it, but you can. However, in order for that to occur, you'll have to recognize that you are guaranteeing the very unhappiness that you don't want.

Q: How am I doing that?

This happiness I'm referring to is not derived from objects or achievements. It is derived from the satisfaction of the desire for the object or achievement. Therefore, happiness is uncovered in the absence of desires.

At present, you are setting yourself up to be unhappy by wrongly defining what makes you happy. For example, if you have money, you are happy and if you don't have money, then you're not happy. You are requiring that a certain condition be present in order for you to be happy. If that condition is absent, you are unhappy.

Q: Well, isn't that how it works?

Not necessarily, but I must admit that it is the most widely accepted viewpoint.

Most unhappiness is a matter of how much of our attention is flowing towards what's not present, what is absent, in our lives. These include desires for certain people, certain conditions, possibly certain objects and certain fantasies. What's paradoxical about it is that, of course, what is desired isn't present. Otherwise, there would be no desire for it. We go about trying to fulfill this or that desire and, even if we succeed, we may find that it's not that great, so we dream up something else we believe will make things better. Or maybe it's everything we hoped it would be. Then, in a day or a month or a year, conditions change and, for whatever reason, it is gone. Now you're back to Square One: unhappy. This is a brutal cycle and unless you end it, it is unending.

Q: Boy, I know that one really well. But, what can I do about it?

There are three levels that you can operate at here. On the more superficial level, I would suggest that you stop wanting what you don't have and want what you have. Stated in a different way, it's also about being happy with What-Is, they way things are. If the universe didn't have to conform to what you imagined it needed to be in every second of every day, where could unhappiness arise from?

On a deeper level, you must come to the recognition that wanting anything that is temporal, fixed in time, is a set-up for unhappiness. This is because all things come and go. That is the nature of the world. They come – you are happy; they leave – you are unhappy. It can also play out in the opposite: persons or situations depart, you are happy; if they return, you are unhappy.

Seeing that "things" are not the answer, one stops pursuing them. There is no longer a desire for happiness because the notion of a desire for happiness is seen to contain an inner contradiction.

At the deepest level, happiness requires no cause; you are already Happiness Itself. This is a happiness that is not conditional on people, objects or situations being a certain way. It is innate, a part of your essential nature. Thinking of unhappiness, all ideas of unhappiness, are movements away from, and obscurations of, this.

Should you doubt me, check and see if you are happy when you are not unhappy.

Q: You're right; this has entirely turned my head around. I really want to look at things differently. Thank you.

You are most welcome. So much energy is expended chasing our desires. Can you imagine how much more energy you'd have available if you wanted nothing?

More Thinking About Thoughts

The thoughts that arise seem to be so much a part of us, don't they? And what would we be without them?

Well, you know, thoughts are not glue; they don't hold you together. Are you worried that you'll fall apart without them? Try this little experiment:

Can you tell me where you store all your problems when you're not thinking about them?

Just for an instant, a nanosecond, did you mind stop as you confronted this? With your thinking in abeyance for this briefest moment, did you collapse, disintegrate or fall apart? Of course not.

Were you there even when your thoughts weren't? Wouldn't that tell you that you are not your thoughts?

Medicine Not for Everybody

Q: What is the general reaction to what you've been saying?
In general, most people are made uncomfortable. The Commander is unwilling to rigorously examine its seeming role as Commander. It's much easier to pooh-pooh it or just walk away.
Q: What about those who are willing to take a look?
Often, it's not easy. We hold onto our little self, and we don't realize that this belief is exactly what brings us our various problems.
Q: But if I decide to hang in there, really hang in there, what's the outcome I should expect?
Boy, you're setting me up with a very loaded question! OK, I'll try to choose my words ever so carefully.
The root illusion is of a "me" that is running the show. The disillusionment that I speak about is the realization that the "me" is the show. This is the end of the false reference point.
When the point of reference is changed, the entire perspective is changed. The video is no longer personal; it's just another video that appears and disappears.
What's the end result? There is no tension with the flow of life. What comes, come; what goes, goes. Everything is accepted and welcomed as only temporary appearances on the grand stage of awareness. There is no drive to infuse it with unnecessary energy.
Q: Could you call it peace?
I would refer to it as the Peace that includes both peace and turmoil. Neither affects it.
Q: Do you mean that I will still get pissed off?
I wouldn't rule it out by offering up some sugar-coated portrait of you sitting in lotus position, eating vegetables and rice, meditating, and looking beatific.
The organism, in all likelihood, will continue to behave as is prescribed by its nature. So, if you were a jerk before.............................
(laughter)

What Are You Really?

Many have come to the conclusion that the separate entity often referred to as the self is an illusion. Denial of the self is the key doctrine of Buddhism, yet it's one of those theories that can't be put into practice in real life, because when applied, it comes close to a paradoxical feedback loop: I believe there is no self; it follows that there is no 'I'; and it follows that nobody believes that there is no 'I'; who is to see this? Why then, does this view, which runs contrary to all of our experience, have appeal? Why, on some deep level, does it resonate?

By labeling the self as an illusion, of course, people do not necessarily mean to suggest that it has no existence at all. They mean that it exists as something other than what it appears to be.

What is meant is that we are not the real source of our decisions or behavior; we just prefer to believe that we are. We are a by-product of the decisions, an epiphenomenon.

Such a view is often reinforced by the observation that our conscious thoughts seem to come from nowhere and then dissolve. You can't catch yourself deciding to think something, however adroit you may be. There is no control over whatever comes, the content merely appears.

This has huge ramifications.

One would suppose that if a decision is conscious there must be immediate consciousness of the decision. But the two are actually distinct.

Unlikely as it seems, contrary to our own impressions yet verified by neuroscience, decisions are actually made slightly before we become aware of them. The length of the delay involved is about a half a second, an observable period of time.

We are anatomically, neurologically, genetically, physiologically no different from apes. If you've seen them in film or at the zoo, you understand what I'm saying.

This begs the question, "Are we merely apes with a software upgrade?" Other serious questions also arise:

Disregarding the way things seem, are we really only passive spectators of the world, simply watching the way we might watch an engaging film?

Do we attribute actions to ourselves that, in fact, are not ours?

If so, who, or more accurately what, is driving this "bus"?

Are we reduced to drones of We Know Not What that is doing we know not what?

These are the BIG questions. However, in order tackle these, we have to have the answers to other questions:

Do you need to think to notice that you are and that you are aware that you are?

Does this sense of presence-awareness come and go, or is it something that is permanent and unmoving?

Whatever appears: thoughts, sensations, feelings, objects……………..are you not the awareness of them?

Did your parents deliberately intend to create this you or was a form merely created through a natural process?

How mechanical is this you; how much of what constitutes this you was installed through genetics and through experience?

Through this line of investigation and inquiry, one gets the answers to the Ultimate Question: What Are You Really

The Ringing of the Bell

Regardless of one's position in life, there seems to be a fundamental desire to better understand one's self and one's relationship with the world in which one lives............ that is to say, you over here and the world over there.

The great good news is that what the mystics have been saying for thousands of years is now receiving confirmation from the quantum physicists and the neuroscientists. It reveals the truth about the lies we tell ourselves.

The bad news is that the good news goes against the entirety of your conditioning, against everything that you've come to believe and hold true. As such, there may arise a resistance to it. That's OK.

No one should simply accept it as gospel. When one takes the time to investigate the matter, to look into it deeply, it often "rings a bell". This ringing of the bell may be postponed by the conditioning, by the acquired belief system of a lifetime. However, its ultimate arrival is inevitable.

What we address in this room is the encouragement to conduct the investigation. It is the support that allows it to remain ongoing, diving deeper and deeper into the limitless expanse of being itself.

Admittedly, this type of inquiry is not for everyone. But for those who are not satisfied with the way things seem to be, you are most cordially invited to participate with us in seeing the way things truly are.

Religion

Q: Where does religion fit in to all this? Does it have a place at all?
All the major religions have sought to express the same message.
However, when the message gets wrapped up in dogma, in ritual, and
in the requirement for intermediaries, the message gets lost.
That message is "there is an essential Oneness from which everything
emerges and to which everything returns". The religions then assign
names to this Oneness and then argue, fight, and kill over whose
Oneness is the only Oneness or the highest Oneness.
The most widely used name is God. I hesitate to use this name because
it has such a polarizing effect on people. But for the sake of answering
your question, I will call this Oneness God.
Now, the religions come along and ask you to believe in God. But what
does it mean to believe? It means to take something as true in the
absence of proof.
As such, although they can't provide proof of this God, they ask for
your belief in It.
Let's step away now from God, so to speak, and return to the notion of
Oneness. As light is the unseen factor in all color, it is clear that some
organizing factor is at work. Your heart beats, the grass grows, the
world functions. I don't have to believe in this organizing factor, it is
obvious.
Q: But there is evil in the world. How do you account for that?
When we speak of beauty, ugliness must already be there so that we
can have a frame of reference for beauty. The label "evil" must already
be there for "goodness" to have any meaning. One is always compared
to the other.
But these labels are relative. What is good today may be bad tomorrow.
What is good for you may be bad for me. The feathers in the empty
cage signify that it was a bad day for the canary but a fine day for the
cat.
All of this manifestation is framed in this polarity of opposites. It is
within the very framework of this polarity that the mind operates.
Q: So you're anti-religion?
I prefer to place the focus on what is agreed upon by all religions, by
what is evident prior to the imposition of any religion. In truth, it
doesn't threaten any religion; it clarifies their core message.

The end result is that one is more religious, with or without religion.
Q: What do you mean "more religious"?
One becomes more aware of the sacredness that envelopes and embraces everything. Following a prescribed religion is not a pre-condition for that.
Q: I don't want to renounce my religion. Yet, if I understand you correctly, that isn't necessary. This can be a complement to my religion.
Quite so. There are many who experience a deepening within their religious experience. Others decide to move away from a particular religion while continuing their exploration into this sacredness.
There is no one-size-fits-all outcome.

Nothing Personal

Q: Is this similar to psychotherapy?

This is the antithesis of psychotherapy. Whereas psychotherapy works to change the person, this point of view gives no attention to this "you" other than to see it as it is: clothing that covers the nakedness of pure aware being.

Turn the clothing upside down and inside out, if you like.... it is still clothing. The person is what appears to be. But, what one is in actuality is far more vast, far more expansive.

Q; Yet, psychotherapy can yield valuable benefits, can't it?

Yes it can, but only to the person. What is this person? The person is the totality of all fears: the fear of pain, the fear of loss, and ultimately, the fear of self-absence. It is the sum of its reactions to external stimuli. These reactions are repetitious and mechanical, a feedback loop in the nervous system.

Too, the person is transitory, coming and going. Where is this person when you are deeply engrossed in a movie or in work? Where is it when you're making love or in awe of a sunset?

Therefore, we don't invest any energy in studying or analyzing the person. We are not trying to make changes to the person. We are trying to shift the fixation from the person to something greater.

Q: Are you saying that the person is unimportant?

The person has its place as a player in the play. It just isn't the area we focus on.

What constitutes a person is in a constant state of changing. What one is today is not what one was 5 years ago. What one was then was not what one was another 10 years before. It's a target that always moving. We prefer to concentrate on what never moves.

Q: What's that?

The undeniable fact of being awareness; one is and one knows one is. What one is..............that's the exciting exploration that is at the root of what I'm speaking about here today.

Q: I don't see how that helps me.

It doesn't help. If helping "you" was the goal, we'd refer this "you" to a psychotherapist.

Freedom

Try as you may, you can never get enough of what doesn't satisfy you. Where do you then turn when "more" is not enough?

Many people may be in touch with the depths of their dissatisfaction and seek out some method, some teacher that will help them. They really aren't seeking change but merely relief. They are going to a restaurant and seeking to satisfy their hunger. I would prefer to give them indigestion, to shake them up in a way that can bring about substantive change, not a mere rearranging of the furniture.

Q: How does this begin?

It begins by your no longer seeking to defend your cage. It is the seeing that the same door that kept you imprisoned is that one that can set you free, that takes you to freedom itself.

Q: This freedom you're talking about, is it the ability to do whatever I want to do?

No, that's simply self-indulgence. This freedom I am speaking about is no longer being dependent on any person or situation for your happiness and well-being.

This is being freed from the world, true freedom. You are no longer hostage to what happens, to who comes or who goes.

You no longer need time because freedom is not some event in the future. Freedom is not tomorrow. That's part of the trap you're already ensnared in; the better tomorrow.

You are also free from authority, from the need for any authority to tell you how to think or how to behave. In this freedom, you are your own authority. Of course, you have to behave within the limits imposed by society as long as you choose to remain in society.

Q; On one level, this makes no sense to me. Yet, somewhere else, it feels as if you've tapped into something very deep inside me.

Please don't take me at my word. I can't swim for you. I can point out how to swim, I can point to the water, but it is you that must dive in.

So, check it out for yourself. In any moment, with whatever comes up, ask yourself "Is this true?"

Q: That's a bit scary. Everything might fall apart.

Admittedly, freedom is scary for a lot of people. It is unknown to them and the known is almost always preferable to the unknown. In that sense, freedom is also release from slavery to the seemingly known.

Q: What's wrong with the known?

The only thing that's "wrong" with the known is that the known, what we think we know, is all-too-often false. Until there is discernment between appearance and reality, you remain ensnared.

Once the discernment occurs, it is like an explosion that blows out the few candles and replaces them with a spotlight.

The Color of the World

When we look at the world through colored glass, we don't see that
world as it truly is. If the glass is yellow, the world appears to be
yellow. Change the glass to pink and the world is markedly different.
It is only when the glass is removed that the actuality can be perceived.
Q: How, then, does a person come to understand the color of the glass,
so to speak, that is in use?
(Laughing) I couldn't have paid you to frame this question in a better
manner.
The person is the color of the glass.
Q: You're saying that my view of the world determines how I
experience the world?
Of course, but there's more. It is not only your view of the world. It is
also how you react to the world. What is a person other than the sum of
the organism's unique reactions to the world?
Q: That really trivializes the whole thing, don't you think?
Not at all. On the contrary, it brings it more in line with the proper
perspective.
Hard-wired for survival, we are always looking at the world to see how
what is going on may impact us. How might your experience of the
world be different if you didn't bring a pre-determined agenda into the
process, if you experienced it from some neutrality, at a distance from
yourself?
Q: I'm not sure.
You're only not sure because you're thoroughly convinced that the way
you experience the world is the only way it can be. You haven't
accepted the possibility of alternatives or of the presence of a subtle bias
that taints it all.
Q: I can concede that. But isn't it possible that if my bias was removed
that the world would appear worse than it is?
In the absence of the bias, in the absence of the personal, the world
doesn't appear worse than it is or better than it is. The world appears as
it is.
Q: I'm not convinced that I'm ready for that.
Don't worry; until you are, nothing will change. What you have been
getting from the world is what you'll continue to get.

Seeing the False as False

The mind has built a structure of concepts about What-Is that bears little relation to actual experience. Through the deconstruction of these concepts, we come to recognize our essence.

These complex and persuasive ideas have put forth an image of ourselves and of the world that is at odds with the facts of our experience. These ideas have convinced us that there is a world that exists separate from and independent of us. They have persuaded us to believe that there is an entity that resides inside the body, that it was born and will die, and that it is the subject of experience while everything else, the world, everything "other", is the object.

At the end of a process of exploring the nature of experience, using the full capacity of its powers to conceptualize, the mind comes to "face-to-face" with the limits of its ability to comprehend this, thereby paving the way for experience to reveal itself to us as it truly is, as in fact it always is, free from the influence and taint of divided, dualistic thinking.

Ultimately, what is revealed is a single, seamless totality, Consciousness and Being, one and the same. The totality of this unfolding, in turn, has a profound impact on the perception of the mind, the body and the world.

Nothing changes, yet everything has changed.

The Way Things Are Not

Q: I have a hard time with the idea that things aren't as they seem to be. Everything feels very real. How can it be otherwise?

Imagine that we were to go to Cancun, Mexico or Fiji. We'd be amazed by the beauty of the turquoise water. I ask you to take a bucket and fill it with the turquoise water because I want to take it home and show it to my friends. Down to the shoreline you go, bucket in hand. When you return, I look in the bucket and with disappointment declare, "This can't be it; the water is clear. Please go and do it again".

Again you go down and again you return with more of the same.............and on and on it goes. How many times do you have to do this until you recognize that the water isn't blue, it is not really as it appears?

Q; I see; you're saying that once I realize this, the water doesn't appear blue anymore?

No, I'm not. What I'm saying is that the water still appears to be blue but you know that it isn't. This knowledge removes all the power from the illusion. Let me give you another example.

Suppose you were in Las Vegas and went to see a performance of Penn and Teller, the illusionists. You sit in the audience and watch Penn shoot a loaded gun at his partner Teller who then catches the bullet in his mouth. Maybe you've really seen them do this.

They take you backstage and show you how the illusion was accomplished and then sit you back down in the audience to watch it again. It looks just like it did before. The difference is that you now have the firm conviction that it's only an illusion. The fixation of attention on it, the mesmerization, is gone. You are now able to see things as they appear yet know things as they really are. You no longer take the appearance for the reality.

Q; I follow you. How is this applied?

It's really all about distinguishing between appearance and reality. I'm not speaking here about some sort of relative reality, my reality or your reality. I'm speaking about a singular reality, the way things truly are.

Q; Sounds interesting; where do we begin?

We begin with this "you" that you think you are.

Clearing Up Problems

Q: A friend of mine said that you were really able to help him with his problems. I was hoping that you could do the same for me. There are so many of them; can you help?

I sure hope so.

When these problems aren't troubling you, where do you keep them?

Q: I'm not sure I understand.

Unless they are troubling you every waking moment of every day, you must put them away somewhere when they aren't an issue. Where do you put them?

Q: I can't say for certain. But I know that they are still in my mind.

OK, so please set your mind out here on the table and let's have a look at it?

Q: I can't do that. I can't just put my mind on the table.

Why not?

Q: I just can't do that.

OK, tell me where it is and I'll do it for you.

Q: It's inside my head.

Where?

Q: I don't know for sure. But that's where it feels like it is.

All right; you believe that it's inside your head but when you look for it, you can't locate it. Maybe it only seems to be inside your head. It would appear logical to assume that it's located there because all of your senses are located in the head. But what if it actually isn't?

Q: I can't say. I'm already becoming perplexed.

Let's move away from where it is for a second and address what it is instead. Mind is thought and thought is mind. There really is no difference, isn't it?

Q: I guess that's right.

Yes, when one is empty of thought, one is said to have an empty mind. Now, coming back, then, to what you said earlier...............there is no place therefore where problems go when they are not troubling you. Either there are thoughts about problems or the problems don't exist.

Q: The problems all seem very real when I am thinking about them. Yet, I never looked at the whole thing quite like this before. But what you say makes sense, it disturbs me to say.

Yes, however one of the things that I hope is becoming clearer for you as we continue to work together is that a lot of reality is not as it seems.

Q: You're then saying that the thought is the core of the problem and not the content of the thought?

In this specific instance, to state it differently, there is nothing wrong unless one thinks about it. So, yes, the thought itself is the problem. In that space.....the nanosecond before one thought departs and another arrives, in that space, nothing can be wrong. In addition, in that same space, you haven't fallen apart, you haven't collapsed in the absence of thought.

As such, thought is not the glue that is holding you together. In truth, thought is closer to that which is tearing you apart.

The Teaching

Q: Do you consider yourself to be a teacher?

The prerequisite for being a teacher is having something to teach. I don't qualify in that sense.

All that I am suggesting is for you to examine these assumptions about yourself that you have carried around for decades.

Q: I've played around with this some and I can see the falseness of many things.

Yes, it is easy to see the falseness of the world yet more difficult to see the falseness of ourselves. Surely, if the world is false, that which is in the world is likewise false.

Q: I'm seeing that we are not separate, that there is an underlying unity amidst all this diversity.

This unity has often been referred to as One Taste. The taste of salt pervades the ocean and every drop of seawater carries that same taste. Likewise, this Complex that I speak about is in all life because it is Life Itself.

The only thing that's separate is the fiction of the individual, this Composite.

Q: Thank you for that confirmation. I will continue to try to get to the heart of the matter.

Why try? Does an orchid try to be beautiful? Beauty is within its very nature. There is nothing it needs to do. Your very nature is this Being Awareness. How hard do you have to try to be that?

The Big Bang Revisited

Once upon a time, in a time before Time, all there was was Awareness; the unified field with the potential for Knowing. When the potential actualized, as would be its inherent nature, duality is born. I am separates into I and am. Conscious Being is now Consciousness and Being. This is the division of the unified field into the Knower and the Known, the self and the world.

Q: This all sounds a bit too cosmic for my tastes. Can you say it in a way that is simpler?

The world you perceive and experience is divided into object, that is the known, and subject, that is the knower. Before that, in the beginning as it were, all that existed was a potentiality. Literally in a finger-snap, the world was born out of it.

Q: Why did it happen?

It is the very nature of potentiality to become. If potential didn't at some time "become", it wouldn't be potential. It would be dead.

Q: Why should I care about any of this?

You operate in the world as something that is outside it. Yet you've never bothered to consider whether that point of view is valid. Neuroscientists have discovered that the brain, as it develops in infancy, concludes that the world outside the body is separate and possibly threatening to the organism that contains it. In order to protect itself, it simulates a self-center from which its negotiations and control can be represented. Of course this simulated individual would appear to have free will, choice and the ability to act.

This entire structure is used to deal with a world that is assumed to be separate. But is there a separate world? Or is the simulation of individuality generated from a false assumption?

This is what we want to look at here.

Q: What's the payoff of all this?

The so-called payoffs can be diverse and numerous.

Many have reported absence of emotional spikes, improved relationships, increased energy, mental clarity, elimination of problems, loss of resentments. The list goes on and on.

One individual may have summed it up best when she said "I no longer desire a better past nor do I fixate on the quality of the future. In fact, nothing is wrong anymore".

Present at Birth

What is left and what is right is relative to where you are. But this left and this right are not the same left and right to the one facing you. It's all only relative to you. Your entire perspective is all relative to this reference point.

Q: I'm still not able to make the distinction between me and this other thing you're talking about.

OK. Are you clear about how this "me" is born at around age 2?

Q: Yes

Good. So what I'm saying is that something was present at your birth despite the fact that this "you" wasn't there. It will likewise be present at your death. What is that? This is the investigation.

Q: This is what you're suggesting I search for?

It is not a thing to search for. It is that through which the search is taking place.

Some notion arose that you are a separate individual with some higher consciousness to be arrived at sometime in the future. The entire notion is false. See the false as false and it falls away.

No Believing, No Accepting

Q: Why should I believe what you have to say?

I am not saying believe what I say, I am not saying accept what I say. I am saying there is no need to be in a hurry to accept or reject. First just hear it, silently with no inner chattering or talk, without evaluating or having to decide.

When you see a beautiful flower or sunset, do you immediately rush to accept or reject it? When you hear wondrous music, do you accept or reject it? You simply stay in it, and in that very staying is an opening.

If what I am saying has any resonance in you, it will be understood. This understanding is not by the mind but by something inherent that resides behind the mind. No action will be required; you will not need to change your life according to it. Life will change of its own accord.

If it doesn't resonate or makes no sense, you'll have ample opportunity to throw it away.

Q: So are you saying just think about it?

It's not even that. I draw the distinction between listening and hearing. Listening can occur while the mind is occupied with other things. But this is superficial. Hearing is listening without all the background noise that the mind can create. Content goes much deeper than in mere listening.

It's more akin to baking bread. You put the material in the oven and let it bake. There's nothing more you need to do.

Q: Are you saying I shouldn't even be taking notes?

Taking notes is a good example of the distractions I'm speaking about. While you're busy taking notes, you're not totally available to hear. You're listening……………that's all.

Q: I'm afraid that if I don't take notes, I'll lose a lot of what you have to say.

That's one way of looking at it. I would prefer that you trust that you'll get what you need to get.

What Does Life Have to Do With It?

Life manifests in infinite ways: as genocides and love affairs, as fields of flowers, as tsunamis, sunlight, eclipses, famines, airplanes flying into towers, births, deaths and on and on.

Each is an individual manifestation within a singular, homogeneous vibrating energy: Life.

The brain, seeking to ensure its continuity, categorizes each event as good/bad, wanted/unwanted, relevant/irrelevant, etc. But all of that is output and it is tainted by the brain's biases.

The input is what makes up perception, sensory cues coming to the processing center...............no opinion, no judgment, no classification. Just what-is, and it is this what-is that is real. What the brain creates is a distortion, a misrepresentation, a belief system. Said system is rooted in the core belief "I am in this body in this world". From there, a vast imagination is spun.

So why do we give credence to the brain's findings? Simply because we don't know any better. No one has come along and told us to question these beliefs.

Even if someone had, most won't do it anyway. It's frightening to consider that one's world may be a sham and it's frightening to understand that one's world is what must be sacrificed for clarity.

The Box

For as long as there is a seeming subject centered within a phenomenal object, and for as long as this seeming subject is identified with that object, true clarity cannot be obtained. How can it be otherwise so long as I am identified with what I am not?

The subjective abandonment of this phenomenal center constitutes the only method; the paradox is that it cannot be performed volitionally. It can only occur.

Understanding this provides the release from all activity crafted to achieve it.

Enlightenment

Q: Would you say that you are enlightened?

If to be enlightened means to be made lighter, then I can probably make that assertion. But if it means that I am some higher being, somehow more evolved, then I am not.

There are no enlightened individuals; in fact, enlightened individuals is an oxymoron just like peace of mind. The mind can never be peaceful and enlightenment is not personal.

Q: Yet, something changes? What changes?

What changes when a migraine goes away?

Q: I don't understand.

The world seen with a migraine is not the same world that is seen without a migraine. The viewpoint is different.

That's the change.

Q: Doesn't sound like much.

Ever had a migraine? (laughter)

Look, enlightenment doesn't mean that overnight you become vegetarian, or that you suddenly find yourself meditating ten hours a day, or that you quit the world and enter a Zen monastery. That's not to suggest that any of these couldn't happen.

My point is that there is no way enlightenment is supposed to look. Each of us may be carrying around images of the way we believe it's supposed to look.

But that's just a peek into that sack of beliefs that each of us is dragging behind us. Ask yourself how many times you may have rejected the message because you found the demeanor of the messenger to be incongruent.

Who said that there had to be congruence between the two?

Q: So you're saying that a murderer could be enlightened?

Again, no one gets enlightened. Enlightenment occurs. The reference point recedes. The life stream continues as before, but there is no longer any preoccupation with how the individual is impacted. From the inside looking out, shit may continue to happen. From the outside looking in, nothing is wrong any more.

Q: Does the ego die?

No. if someone were to call out "Roy", I would still turn my head toward them in response. I still feel the pulls of emotion. Roy continues on; I've simply realized that he's not what I am in essence. Roy is now seen as a TV channel. I can tune it in or I can tune it out.

Whether or not I'm tuned into that station, the life stream continues. When I'm tuned into Roy, that is to say when I'm involved, life can at times seem tumultuous. When I tune out the narrative of Roy, life flows more smoothly.

Q: Why?

Why not?

Q: So are you saying that if I ignore my life, I'll be happier?

What I am saying is that once you see this life without the reference point, the quality of your participation in it is altered.

You understand that you are no longer confined to be being a body in the world. You are no longer a tenant.

You've become the landlord.

The Seamless Web

A hologram is a three- dimensional photograph made with a laser. To make a hologram, the object to be photographed is first bathed in the light of a laser beam. Then a second laser beam is bounced off the reflected light of the first and the area where the two laser beams co-mingle is captured on film. When the developed film is illuminated by another laser beam, a three-dimensional image of the original object appears.

Now, here's what is truly remarkable about holograms. If a hologram of a tulip is cut in half and then illuminated by a laser, each half will still be found to contain the entire image of the tulip. Even if the halves are divided again, each fraction of film will always be found to contain a smaller but intact version of the original image. Every part of a hologram contains all the information possessed by the whole.

This whole in every part quality of holograms provides us with an entirely new way, a game-changing way, of looking at things.

If every thing contains everything, then the apparent separateness is illusory. This means that at a deeper level, all things are interconnected. Although humans may label, categorize and divide all phenomena, these attempts mask the truth. All of nature is ultimately a single, seamless web.

Too, if things only appear separate, if their separateness is an illusion, then there are no individual entities. There are only extensions of the same fundamental intelligence energy, working in consort with one another.

Holograms also possess an astounding capacity for information storage. If you simply change the angle at which the two lasers strike a piece of photographic film, it is possible to record many different images on the same surface. It has been demonstrated that one cubic centimeter of film can hold as many as 10 billion bits of information.

The hologram can then be seen to be a sort of storage facility for All There Is…………….. and within that All There Is, it would make perfect sense that the past, present, and the future are all contained in it too.

Our ability to quickly retrieve whatever information we need from the enormous store we possess becomes more understandable if we look at brain function as holographic.

If a friend asks what comes to mind when he says the word giraffe, you don't have to laboriously sort through some gigantic, cerebral file to arrive at an answer. Instead, associations like tall, orange, and animal native to Africa all pop up instantly.

In the human's processing of information, every piece seems instantly cross- referenced with every other piece. This is another intrinsic aspect of holograms; it confirms a vast body of scientific evidence that suggests that the brain uses holographic principles to perform its operations.

But where does this leave us?

It leaves us as receivers, if you will, awash in a kaleidoscope of energetic vibrations, wherein our holographic brain taps into a single channel of broadcast and transforms it into the physical reality we perceive.

The Payoff

Q: When this pursuit is over, will I have found all the answers?

I can't say it as such. I would prefer to say that you are left without questions. Lacking questions, no answers are needed.

Q: But you will be proven right?

In the end, all is known directly, no proofs are therefore required. Every moment carries the taste of infinity, of limitlessness, in the same way as every drop of the ocean carries the taste of salt.

Q: Will there be discernible changes in me?

I can't say whether or not they will be discernible You will have shifted your focus from definitions and descriptions to what is indefinable and indescribable.

Q: That feels like a huge change. As things are right now, you and I are quite different.

Not as much as you think. You are concerned with the future; my concerns are solely now. I am content with observing and have relinquished the idea of being an actor. I am free.

Q: You're free from what?

To be free means to be free from events, to be OK with whatever comes and whatever departs. To be free is to be free from preferences.

Q: Are you free from the world as Jesus suggested we should be?

The world is like my shadow; it follows me wherever I go. I recognize it to be equally as real.

Q: Why is the world the way it is?

The world is the way it is because you are the way you are. Your world is of your own creation.

The "seeing" and "hearing" that we attribute to our eyes and ears is really the result of the brain processing sketchy and limited data of the outside world that is sensed, captured, and transmitted to it. The brain forms the experiences that you become aware of by taking this incomplete sensory data, looking for patterns that match previous experiences, making inferences to fill in the holes of missing data or unexpected patterns, before integrating the different inputs into what we assume to be a unified awareness.

Your brain processes about 400 billion bits of information every second. Usually, however, you are conscious of only about 2,000 of those bits of data. You believe that reality is where your attention is in any moment. However, the placement of attention forces the brain to exclude vast amounts of incoming data. So, it can't be representing reality. It represents the way things seem to it.

Q: The promise of what you're talking about holds great appeal for me. Yet, you've suggested that most people have no interest in this line of investigation.

If the brain can't predict how an experience will feel, because we lack any related past memories that have already been experienced as a set of feelings, we are more than likely to avoid engaging in that experience. It's one of the downsides of human nature.

It's the same thing with the almost universal discomfort with change. The demand for permanence is really a subtle demand for repetition. We don't want the not known, we only want the already known.

Q: So the bottom line is that we're slaves to our brains?

We are our brains. What else? The myriad facets of our behavior, thoughts, and experience are inseparably yoked to the brain and to the nervous system. We don't understand it; however, we are it.

The brain is an incredible instrument. I am not in any way disparaging the brain. But we must acknowledge the way things are. The brain has its own shadow.

The center of reference created by self consciousness arising from the brain is the so-called me. The interior dialogue, is the "hearing" of the brain talking. But that which is conscious of the brain "talking" is not in the brain. It supports the brain and all its activities.

Q: And the mind?

The mind is nothing apart from its content, the continuous stream of thoughts.

Q: And the personality?

Personality is this set of memories, behaviors, values, beliefs, perceptions, and attitudes that we project into the world or hide from the world. It points back to the brain. It is the style of the brain, so to speak.

Q: Then we're stuck.

Not at all. I've pointed the way out.

You stop pushing on the door that opens inward. To be a person is to be self conscious; yet, we are not self conscious every moment of every day. Therefore, the person is transient.

What are you in those intervals in between experiencing yourself as a person?

The answer gets you unstuck.

Virtuality

The world simulation constantly being created by our brains is built around a center as the reference point. We create the robust feeling of being in direct contact with the outside world by simultaneously generating an ongoing "out-of-brain experience" and a sense of immediate contact with your "self." At the very moment we wake up in the morning, the system starts this process.

It is little more than shadow. The shadow is there. It is real to the extent that you can see it, but it is an illusion in the sense that it has no independent existence.

This process is necessary so that the world makes sense. We, at times, add details, omit facts, or even invent perceptions that are not at all true.

The brain constantly makes assumptions about what exists and what doesn't. Sometimes the assumptions are correct. Other times they aren't.

This phenomenality is the world we are present and immersed in. It fits the definition of a virtual reality.

The Last Word (for now)

All these movies that we refer to as our story all end the same way: The theater goes dark and the viewer exits the structure.

Epilogue

I went to visit Roy (that mover and shaker). But when I got there, his seat was empty. What I discovered instead was this inscription:

Wonder
Ponder
See.
Never before
Never again
Never not.
Now
Here
Always present.
Present
Always
Already
Only this.

Printed in Great Britain
by Amazon.co.uk, Ltd.,
Marston Gate.